SUCCESSFUL FACULTY EVALUATION PROGRAMS

A Practical Guide to Improve Faculty Performance *and* Promotion/Tenure Decisions

Peter Seldin

Pace University
Pleasantville, New York

COVENTRY PRESS
Crugers, New York 10521

© Copyright 1980 by Peter Seldin

All rights reserved. Readers are welcome to use the following forms or items from them without requesting permission from the author: Numbers 2, 4, 5, 7, 8, 9, 10, 11, 13, 14, and 16.

No other forms or items from them or other parts of this book may be reproduced or transmitted in any form or by any means, electronic or mechanical including photocopy, recording, or any information storage or retrieval system, without permission in writing from the author.

Library of Congress Catalog Card Number: 79-67591

First Printing, January, 1980

Second Printing, January, 1981

Printed in the United States of America

Cover designed by Oni

The Author

Peter Seldin is Professor of Management at Pace University, Pleasantville, New York, where his principal teaching area is human and organizational behavior. Formerly Associate Dean at Fordham University, he has been on both sides of the faculty evaluation process.

He has written two previous books, *How Colleges Evaluate Professors* (1975) and *Teaching Professors to Teach* (1977) and is a frequent contributor of articles on faculty development and evaluation in such publications as *The New York Times* and *Change Magazine*.

Presenter of numerous conference papers and workshops in this country and abroad, Peter Seldin is a member of the Program Advisory Council of the International Conference on Improving University Teaching.

To Pat,
  Marc, Amy, Nancy

CONTENTS

Preface

Few issues in higher education spark as much heat as the evaluation of faculty performance. Everyone in academe seems to have an opinion—often biased by personal experiences—but few claim the necessary detachment for an in-depth understanding of the subject.

To provide just such an understanding is the purpose of *Successful Faculty Evaluation Programs*. Its goal is improving instructor performance. To support this objective, the book provides numerous practical strategies, sample appraisal forms and specific guidelines. Seven separate areas of faculty evaluation are discussed: student, colleague and self-assessment, student learning, student advising, institutional service and research and publication. The book is designed to help professors and administrators avoid the pitfalls and develop the requisite skills and sensitivity for a successful evaluation program.

Successful Faculty Evaluation Programs is intended to serve as a practical resource in developing and upgrading programs for instructor evaluation. Each of the guidelines, forms and strategies has been field-tested and adjusted for workability.

To provide a national framework to institutions setting up new programs, Chapter Two provides key findings of the writer's 1978 survey of 678 public and private colleges and their faculty appraisal practices. And four models, in successful use today, are described in Chapter Nine.

This book, like nearly all others, is not solely attributable to its author. Each of the following people has been a ready source of advice and encouragement and deserve special thanks: Derek Bok, Harvard: John Centra, Educational Testing Service; Kenneth Eble, University of Utah; Jerry Gaff, Society for Values in Higher Education; Anthony Grasha, University of Cincinnati; Christopher Knapper, University of Waterloo (Canada); Benjamin Massey, University of Maryland; Wilbert McKeachie, University of Michigan; David Warren Piper, University of London (England); Albert Smith, University of Florida and Robert Wilson, University of California, Berkeley.

Richard Miller, State University of New York at Brockport, contributed the introduction and has been particularly helpful throughout this project.

JJS and RES continue to be strong sources of encouragement for my writing. Pat, my wife, has been especially supportive and understanding of the many hours spent on this book. Marc, Amy and Nancy, our children, followed this project with avid interest and contributed a valuable sense of balance to my life.

Pleasantville, New York   Peter Seldin

Introduction

I am pleased to write a few words before the main event, which of course is the book itself. Before turning to the book, something about the national context would seem in order. What is happening in the area of faculty evaluation? These observations are offered about the past seven years.

1. The interest in faculty evaluation continues to increase. I thought that this interest might peak by now but this has not happened. The rate of increase is slower than in the early and mid-70s, however. Higher education is considerably more sophisticated about faculty evaluation than was the case in 1972. Research and development have greatly expanded our base of theoretical and applied knowledge. Sophistication, properly used, can provide better programs; improperly used, it turns toward cynicism or inactivity.

2. The uses made of faculty evaluation programs are receiving greater scrutiny than in the past. In some cases, union contracts specify the nature of the faculty evaluation; in other contracts the matter is dealt with in a very general manner. The use of faculty evaluation results in increasingly rigorous procedures for making promotion and tenure decisions is causing greater scrutiny, bringing about modifications in faculty evaluation procedures in many cases and discarding the program in some cases. But usually something arises from these ashes that is an improvement. Where nothing arises, however, evaluation must rely upon a narrow spectrum of more subjective and speculative judgment.

3. Faculty evaluation and faculty development have become more closely related, and this is desirable. Professional development programs must mesh with faculty evaluation if faculty development is to have authentic, positive results.

4. The fourth generalization, closely related to number three, is that faculty evaluation is being seen in broader contexts. Faculty development is one such broader context; institutional vitality, instructional improvement, and program development are others.

5. A number of excellent evaluation programs/systems are now available. Some of these are commercial, some are system-wide, some are single campus based. The choice is considerably greater than seven years ago. A word of caution may be in order, however. Salesmanship of systems is no substitute for careful scrutiny at the system or campus level as to real needs and available resources.

6. Evaluation in the broader context—students, administrators, programs, and institutions—is receiving greater attention than seven years ago. For example, the "pass-fail" surge in course evaluation has largely subsided from its high water mark about five years ago. Brown University, a national leader in this effort then, has quietly moved back to more traditional grading. The overall thrust toward more rigorous evaluation cuts across the institution in many ways. And the greater decline in enrollments ahead for many colleges and universities indicates that we can expect increased evaluative efforts in the next seven years.

Peter Seldin has written an excellent book that will be a major contribution to the field of faculty evaluation. Building upon his previous research, study, and practice, he has produced a volume that combines theory with practice in a meaningful manner.

The comprehensive nature of Dr. Seldin's effort will be helpful to those who are considering a comprehensive evaluation system, those who are repairing their systems, and those who are evaluating what is in place. While it is difficult to single out particular treatments because I find the book uniformly of high quality, some aspects do stand out. The survey results provide fresh data and insights into faculty evaluation for private and public liberal arts colleges, and the comparisons of data over time is particularly useful.

The section on "common objections to student ratings" meets these major criticisms effectively. Too often a tendency exists to avoid the arguments of those who oppose or criticize student ratings. And there are some legitimate weaknesses in the best student rating systems that need to be addressed. Peter Seldin does this.

The book contains sample forms that can be useful. The motto, "Adapt rather than adopt" applies to all forms, however. Those presented in this book provide a good basis for such adaptations.

The chapter on "self-evaluation" is the best treatment of this subject that I have seen. The area has not received the attention that it deserves, and Dr. Seldin's chapter can serve to stimulate greater activity in this area.

The next chapter on "student learning" analyses uses student learning as a measure of teaching effectiveness. The sciences have been most supportive of this area because the quantifiable nature of the science disciplines lend themselves to this treatment.

The chapter on "student advising and institutional service" provides an excellent discussion of this important area. Interest in better advising has increased substantially in recent years— probably as much a reaction to the economic motivations of retention as anything else. But in any case, Seldin's treatment of this area provides useful material for those who would evaluate the quality of student advising.

The book brings the research and practice of faculty evaluation up-to-date, and provides many insights that will be provocative and useful to anyone interested in this important and sensitive matter.

Richard I. Miller

Chapter 1

What's Involved in Evaluating Faculty Performance

The Recent Past

The illusion spread across the nation in the sixties that colleges and universities were as fiscally sound as the nation's major corporations. This optimism engendered academic budgetary largesse, ready and ample funding for research, and the emergence of an aggressive breed of academic recruiting officers who located and enticed talent to fill the brand new faculty positions that were being created. New classroom buildings, laboratories and dormitories were rapidly constructed to meet the needs of a huge and rising number of students. To pay for the new construction, the institutions borrowed heavily, dipped into their endowments and raised tuition sharply. In surprising fashion, little or no attention was given to any cost-benefit analyses, student enrollment projections for the seventies, or other customary long-range planning.

The financial pinch arrived in 1970, with a declining rate of income growth and rising costs that seemed uncontrollable. An unfortunate number of colleges and universities kept alive the illusion of growth by resorting to unsophisticated enrollment projections and by serious underestimates of the growth and impact of community colleges.

The near panic was on as the squeeze on college and university budgets tightened. With stepped up inflation, the prices paid for goods and services by the institutions jumped dramatically. Between 1971 and 1978, for example, these prices rose 56.5 percent and construction costs were up 71.5 percent, according to the higher education price index developed by the National Institute for Education. The most volatile component in the rising costs was utilities. For every $100 spent on electricity, fuel and other such utilities in 1967, the institutions spent $292.50 in 1978.

As if inflation was not trouble enough, the federal government added to the institutions' woes by a sharp cutback of subsidies, on which many institutions depended for solvency. The financial health of many colleges and universities became frail indeed.

In 1971 the situation deteriorated to the point where the Carnegie

1

Commission on Higher Education concluded by projection that two-thirds of all the colleges and universities were mired in serious financial problems or would be in the immediate future.

In the heady search for survival, many institutions turned anxiously to intensive self-examination. Most saw salvation only in vigorous fund-raising activities and relentlessly pursued any potential donor. A few turned to speculative ventures in real estate, or the stock market. Grinnell College, in Iowa, one of the nation's most respected liberal arts colleges, invested a sizable portion of its endowment in the purchase of a $13,000,000 commercial television station.

Several institutions decided to *reduce* their tuition rates in an attempt to attract more students. Vermont College cut its tuition by $200 to avoid a drop in enrollment, while Regents of the University of Wisconsin voted to cut out-of-state tuition by 40 percent in an attempt to attract more students to the Platteville campus from nearby areas of Iowa and Illinois.

The smaller private colleges specially hitched their survival directly to the production of more tuition income by the attraction of more students. These institutions decided to face head-on the problems of shrunken enrollments and inflated deficits by the bold use of marketing techniques. They included hard sell on radio, television and by direct mail. They also included ambitious marketing surveys whose findings were applied by the initiation of new programs and the repositioning of the institutions in the academic marketplace. Some colleges hired consulting firms to reorganize and even run the admissions office. Others employed public relations specialists to try to project a more enticing image to consumers.

In the frenetic race to solvency, many institutions turned on themselves and scrutinized the efficiency of their own fiscal management. They hurriedly introduced modern management techniques, which included cost-benefit analyses and a line-by-line examination of expenditure and income.

Since higher education is a labor-intensive industry (70 to 80 percent of typical budgets goes for salaries), where expenses have consistently outpaced the cost of living, it was natural for institutions to look on the instructional staff as a fertile area to reduce costs. One way was to increase the number of students per faculty member and the number of courses acceptable as a full-time teaching load. Another way was to encourage experimenting with different modes of instruction to discover the most cost-efficient. A great many institutions pruned the number of courses by fixing a minimum number of students for undergraduate classes.

The high cost of tenure (at some institutions over 70 percent) was deftly skirted by many institutions by the simple device of hiring more part-time faculty. Since part-time instructors can be hired when needed and dropped when not, and earn less salary and fewer benefits than full-time instructors, the savings to the institution were considerable. The practice of hiring part-time instructors began to flourish.

By hiring part-time faculty to non-tenure track positions, colleges and universities sharply reduced their current costs and hedged against the uncertainties of the 1980's.

For some institutions, recognition of their precarious financial position came too late. Unable to boost income and cut costs sufficiently, some 80 liberal arts colleges have been forced to close their doors since 1970.

At the same time that colleges and universities were exploring income-producing and cost-cutting techniques, they were called to task by community and governmental demands that professors be held accountable for their teaching performance. This pressure for teaching accountability reached as high as the national level. In a stinging critique, Dr. Terrance Bell, the newly appointed Commissioner of Education in 1974, said: "Education is not sufficiently performance conscious. Because it is hard to measure performance, we have almost abandoned the task. Every key person...at a college should know what the objectives and priorities are before each academic year begins."

Discovering how faculty members use their time became of burgeoning interest to state legislatures which funded the public colleges and universities. In Texas, for example, all 31 senior public colleges and universities were directed by a 1977 state law to submit reports on the percent of professional time and salary devoted to teaching, related administration, and other professional assignments. In Kentucky, criticism by state officials that the Kentucky State University was a "high-cost institution," induced the university's board of regents to impose a freeze on the granting of faculty tenure.

Soon the demand for faculty accountability became a groundswell movement across the nation. It enlisted taxpayers, institutional trustees, financial donors and students to pressure colleges and universities to examine the cost-effectiveness of each department and the performance of each professor.

In the public eye, and under the financial gun, the colleges and universities had to face up to excruciating personnel decisions. Who on the faculty was to be promoted, who granted tenure, who terminated? The need for broader and more accurate data on which

3

such decisions could be made became critical. At almost all universities, effective evaluation of faculty performance became the top priority.

Evaluation to Improve Performance

Evaluation of faculty performance is hardly new. It has always had a place in academic history, if only by inference or casual observation. Students have always come up with an appraisal of the teacher's effectiveness and passed such appraisal on to other students. Faculty members pick up impressions of a colleague's competence and exchange their views with their peers at teachers' gatherings. What is new is the attempt to root out casual bias, hearsay evidence and gossip—the traditional hallmarks of organizations—in favor of a systematic evaluation of faculty performance.

Why the needed change? In the long run the dominant reason is to lend a more objective hand to assist an instructor to improve his teaching performance. Just as students need feedback to correct errors, faculty members need more factual data to point the direction to self-improvement. The word "dissonance" is commonly applied as the key reason for a teacher to want to improve his performance. It is held that the feedback from a range of evaluations can produce in the teacher the kind of dissonance or dissatisfaction that sets the psychological stage for change.

Whether such improvement actually takes place, however, depends in large measure on the kind of facts turned up by the evaluations. It won't work unless the instructional element or elements to be improved are specifically singled out. And even then, as Goldschmidt (1977) has pointed out, the teacher must genuinely care about the evaluative process, and realistically be able to make the change, to produce the improvement.

Despite the dearth of studies on the effects of giving professors feedback on their performance, it appears safe to assert that simply handing a professor the results of, say, student evaluations will probably fall short of motivating self-improvement. A follow-up injection of short periods of faculty counseling may be needed.

As a consequence, many colleges and universities have set up faculty development centers, staffed by instructional consultants, to bring advice and guidance to faculty members interested in converting evaluative feedback into teaching improvement. A teacher asking for help will work one-to-one with a consultant. Feedback on his teaching performance will come from many sources: a sample of instructional material, classroom observation, a videotaped classroom session, student evaluation, instructor self-assessment. After a joint analysis by the consultant and the faculty member, the teaching skill or skills needing improvement will be

4

identified and corrective action planned.

Question—does faculty evaluation actually result in improved performance? The evidence is murky. Centra (1977, p. 104) surveyed faculty development directors at 756 colleges and universities and found that, "Between 40 to 60 percent of the respondents saw the evaluation process as being effective in improving teaching. . . ." Centra cautioned, however, that the survey respondents' views "may be based less on hard evidence than on general optimism."

The Massachusetts Advisory Council on Education (1975, p. 9) found that helping faculty to improve performance, although on the top of the list of intended purposes of faculty evaluation, "typically falls short as a demonstrated accomplishment."

The Southern Regional Educational Board (1977, p. 14) observed that although "many think the results of faculty evaluation programs should be used as a basis for faculty development and improvement, the results are used instead primarily for making personnel decisions."

Evaluation for Personnel Decisions

Another reason for assessing faculty performance is to provide a rational, equitable basis for crucial administrative decisions on tenure, promotion in rank and retention. These decisions have always been made by colleges and universities. But in recent years, under growing pressure, many institutions have moved faculty evaluation for personnel decisions on the top of the list of reasons for assessing performance.

Granting tenure has serious financial implications. It can commit an institution to a salary that can exceed $600,000 over a 30-year period. For good reason, standards for tenure are more rigorous today in institutions of higher learning. Some institutions have even moved to impose percentage limits on tenured faculty.

In addition, many institutions, facing tenure decisions, are demanding more than the traditional evidence on research, publication and service to the institution and community. They are now evaluating teaching performance. At Harvard University, for example, for the first time, a systematic evaluation of teaching skills has been accorded a crucial role in tenure decisions. At Stanford University, after two candidates who had received campus awards for distinguished teaching were denied tenure, embarrassed officials accepted a task force's recommendations that the teaching in each course be evaluated regularly.

In the pursuit of sound administrative decisions, many colleges and universities have moved quickly to evaluate faculty performance. In haste, some inaccurate data-gathering methods and instruments have been adopted with the inevitable result of flawed decisions. Contemporary practices on too many campuses are marred by a feverish rather than deliberative approach to evaluation.

In general, faculty members are the first to concede that dead wood needs elimination from their ranks, but they balk at what they consider a non-objective screening process. It is a truism that few teachers regard themselves as departmental dead wood. But almost every faculty member has a sense of unease about his ranking in relation to his colleagues.

Evaluation for Guiding Students

An additional reason for measuring faculty performance is to provide students with a handy guide for the selection of courses and instructors. The outburst of student militancy in the late sixties produced a flowering of programs which enable students to rate courses and instructors. The student ratings are typically printed in a serviceable handbook for other students. At times the ratings are supplemented by teacher comments on the goals and workload of the courses. But to lend balance to the handbook, and increase its usefulness to students in making course and instructor decisions, faculty and administrative assistance is vital.

When conducted by students alone, the ratings have a tendency at times to convert the handbook into appraisals written in vitriol. That is both unfortunate and unnecessary and does disservice to students and teachers alike. Occasionally, some faculty members, citing damage to their professional reputations, take legal action to force students to issue public apologies and destroy undistributed copies of a handbook. Handbooks are best when they are the joint effort of students, faculty and administrators.

Evaluation to Provide Data to Outsiders

Still another reason for assessing faculty performance is to be able to provide data to interested individuals and organizations operating off the campus. Taxpayers, parents, government officials, boards of trustees and a wide range of advocacy groups have demanded all sorts of data on institutional and faculty efficiency. In a number of states, legislation requires colleges and universities to prepare and maintain detailed records on hiring, promotion, tenure and retention.

Pointedly, the Massachusetts Advisory Council on Education (1975, p. 10) says that institutions keeping a good set of records may actually have a better chance of surviving in the hot competition in higher education. The Council recommends that institutions on their own initiative "collect and disseminate overall effectiveness information (on) students served, student learning and satisfaction ratings, drop-out and matriculation rates, alumni employment and achievement patterns, community and social contributions...."

Barriers to Evaluating Performance

To say that evaluation of faculty performance is useful is one thing, to get the evaluation system off the ground is another. First, is the immediate problem of developing accurate measuring rods of faculty performance. This is no simple matter. But it is disheartening to see how the rash use of unreliable methods, vague criteria, and uncertain performance standards, have undermined academic faith in faculty evaluation. Just because the measurement of performance is inherently difficult is not reason to consider the problem insurmountable and therefore rejectable. This reasoning makes it easy to rationalize away the need for faculty appraisal.

Second, there are social and attitudinal problems. Some academics persist in the argument that direct observation, even by qualified personnel using acceptable tools of measurement, is an invasion of professional privacy. They argue that the teacher is entitled to autonomy in a classroom. Priest (1967, p. 287) disposes of this argument: "Evaluation is an inherent element of any organized effort to achieve a goal. We must submit to and cooperate with rational types of evaluation or be evaluated by ludicrously shoddy means. A large percentage of professors have convinced each other that they are unique and therefore not subject to evaluation. This is sophistry."

Other opponents of evaluation argue that teaching is too complex and subjective to be evaluated. McKeachie (1967, p. 211) responds that "it is the very complexity of the teaching situation that makes every bit of empirical information the more precious." On the same point, Gustad (1961, p. 2) concludes from his study of faculty evaluative practices in 584 colleges and universities, that, "A perfectly reliable and valid system of evaluation may, in fact, be for the foreseeable future unattainable; nevertheless ... given time, effort, and the kind of critical appraisal that identifies blind alleys, reasonable approximations to a goal can be obtained."

No one will argue that absolute precision and objectivity in evaluation is foreseeable. But to eliminate faculty appraisal because today's techniques of getting at it are imperfect is not an answer. A candle light is more helpful in finding our way than total darkness. Two candles will be better. The object is to add candles and steadily and collectively increase the illumination.

Beneath the surface reasons against faculty appraisal lies the unspoken professorial dislike of being judged. This is natural. The professor, like most human beings, tends to regard an appraisal as an implicit threat. No one wants to be threatened unnecessarily. Centra (1977, p. 93), in recognition of this deep motivation, observes: "Since evaluation can be threatening and ill-defined and can sometimes result in unfair judgments, their reluctance is understandable."

This natural resistance needs sympathetic understanding and a trade-off approach that emphasizes the positive values to the professor in teaching improvement. Futhermore, since evaluation is almost inevitable, in the higher education realities of today, it is patently better to be judged systematically and with reasonable justice than by the haphazard and whimsical methods of the past.

Less sympathy is due the handful of diehards who have deliberately slowed the development of appraisal techniques by stonewall opposition. Dressel (1959) charges them with interpreting academic freedom as inclusive of the privilege to teach us badly as they wish. They prefer to cloak their teaching performance from scrutiny which raises the suspicion that the performance may need hiding. The sooner they are forced to put aside their cloaks, and any teaching deficiencies revealed, the better. At the very least, the suspicion will be laid to rest.

What is Effective Teaching?

Some faculty members oppose ratings by students, peers or anyone else, on the ground that the characteristics of effective teaching are too elusive to measure. How can effective teaching be evaluated, they argue, when no one truly knows what effective teaching is?

These faculty members unwittingly dismiss the huge and growing number of scholarly investigations that are sorting out effective and ineffective teaching behavior. Dunkin and Biddle (1974) have added up more than 10,000 published studies on one phase or another of teaching effectiveness. From this body of research arise reasonably consistent findings on what constitutes effective teaching.

No one doubts that we are short many answers to the teaching-learning process, just as we still have missing pieces to the cancer puzzle. But we do have some of the answers. And, as Hildebrand (1975, p. 31) remarks, "the concept of effective teaching is more exact than those of beauty, love, morality, femininity, normality, perversion, good taste, God, and many more." Difficult to define and measure, yes, but they are in our everyday vocabulary and we do not hesitate to use them because they lack neat definitions.

In the past fifty years, a number of research methods have been used to identify some characteristics of good teaching. These include observational analysis, correlation studies, factor analysis

8

and the critical incident approach.

Piper (1977, pp. 7, 14, 16) describes three dominant factors uncovered in his own research that make for effective teaching.

GIVING THE OPPORTUNITY TO LEARN

Subject expertise
Clear criteria of learning
Choice of teaching method
Expertise in use of teaching method
Timetabling
Facilities management

IMPROVING THE ABILITY TO LEARN

Teacher acts as a 'process consultant'
An understanding of the mental process of learning.
Ways of helping student develop "learning abilities".
Expertise in making interventions in the student's learning
    process.
Organized view of the skills and habits which enhance academic
    work.
Identification of key 'facilitating objectives' and a systematic way
    of teaching the student how to achieve them.
Establishing an effective means of communication between
    student and staff which allows access to the student's learning
    process.

IMPROVING THE INCENTIVE TO LEARN

Clear briefing of students.
Agreements on purposes and methods.
Means of analyzing purposes of assessment.
Repertoire of assessment methods.
Evaluation of assessment.
Expertise in human relations.
Counselling—knowing when to refer to a specialist.

Perry (1969), as part of a study for the University of Toledo's Office of Institutional Research, examined *faculty* perceptions of effective teaching. Six characteristics led the list. They were: (1) being well prepared for class, (2) demonstrating comprehensive subject knowledge, (3) encouraging intelligent, independent thought by students, (4) motivating students to do their best, (5) being fair and reasonable in evaluating students, (6) being sincerely

9

interested in the subject being taught.

Student perceptions of effective teaching were examined by Eble (1970, pp. 99-100), in a study completed by the Center for Research and Development in Higher Education at Berkeley. From the students' side, a good teacher (1) is a dynamic and energetic person, (2) explains clearly, (3) has an interesting style of presentation, (4) seems to enjoy teaching, (5) has a genuine interest in students and is friendly toward them, (6) encourages class discussions, (7) discusses points of view other than his own.

Seldin (1975), in a study of 410 *academic deans'* views of good teaching, worthy of contract renewal and promotion in rank, finds the same high store placed on the same characteristics. An effective teacher (1) is well prepared for class, (2) motivates students to do their best, (3) communicates effectively to the level of the students, (4) demonstrates comprehensive subject knowledge, (5) treats students with respect.

Employing factor analysis—a method of statistical analysis which establishes the tendency of responses to cluster, e.g., items on a rating scale—Irby (1978) analyzed sixteen studies dealing with students' perceptions of teachers. He found a heavy cluster response on four points. They are: (1) organization/clarity, (2) enthusiasm/ stimulation, (3) instructor knowledge, (4) group interactional skill. The results of his research are in Figure 1.

Even though no single list of teaching qualities has yet been developed to everyone's satisfaction, it seems clear that the general characteristics of effective teaching are emerging.

In a review of studies going back to the beginning of this century, Eble (1976, p. 18) notes "reasonably consistent findings about the earmarks of good teaching." In a summary he says:

Most studies stress knowledge and organization of subject matter, skills in instruction, and personal qualities and attitudes useful to working with students.

If personal characteristics are emphasized in a particular study, good teachers will be singled out as those who are enthusiastic, energetic, approachable, open, concerned, imaginative, and possessed of a sense of humor.

If characteristics of mastering a subject matter and possessing teaching skills are emphasized, good teachers will be those who are masters of a subject, can organize and emphasize, can clarify ideas and point out relationships, can motivate students, can pose and elicit useful questions and examples, and are reasonable, imaginative, and fair in managing the details of learning.

10

Figure 1.
Apparent similarities of dimensions found in
16 factor analyses of instructor ratings

Dimensions	Organization/ Clarity	Enthusiasm/ Stimulation	Instructor Knowledge	Group Instructional Skill
Studies				
Isaacson et al. (1964)	Structure	Skill		Rapport
Solomon, Rosenberg, and Bezdik (1964)	Clarity, expressive-ness vs obscurity, vagueness	Energy vs. lethargy		Lecturing vs. encouragement of student participation
Solomon (1966)	Precision/ organization vs. informal-ity, obscur-ity; Difficulty of presentation vs. clarity	Energy, facility of communica-tion vs. lethargy, vagueness	Control, factual emphasis vs. per-missive-ness	Warmth, approval vs. coldness; Lecturing vs. encouragement of broad, ex-pressive student participation
Deshpande, Webb, and Marks (1970)	Cognitive merit	Stimulation		Affective merit
Turner (1970)	Penetrating, clear, focused	Exciting, humorous, stimulating	Prepared, probing, demanding	Approachable, warm, cheer-ful
Hildebrand, Wilson, and Dienst (1971)	Organization/ clarity	Dynamism/ enthusiasm	Analytic/ synthetic approach	Instructor/ group interaction
Frey (1973)	Organization/ clarity	Teacher's presentation		Teacher accessibility
McKeachie and Lin (1973)	Structure	Skill		Group Inter-action
Blazek (1974)	Instructor clarity	Instructor knowledge/ enthusiasm	Instructor knowledge/ enthusiasm	Instructor openness
Pohlmann (1975)	Organized in presenting material	Increases student's appreciation of the sub-ject matter		
Rugg and Norris (1975)	Structure and Guidance	Stimulating teaching	Subject matter expertise; Research methods expertise	Interpersonal rapport, respect for students

Source: Adapted from Irby (1978)

11

Some faculty members oppose evaluation on the ground that members of the academic community disagree on the identification of effective and ineffective instructors. Students, faculty and alumni, they argue, see different teaching behaviors as important.

In his study, Perry (1969) asked almost 2,000 students, faculty and alumni to rank the importance of sixty teaching characteristics. Considerable agreement turned up among all the participants.

Kulik (1974) also finds general agreement on teacher ratings whether done by faculty colleagues or by students. He also reports that teacher ratings by college administrators are practically interchangeable with those of the teacher's colleagues.

Hildebrand (1975), in a comparison of student and faculty perceptions of the best and worst teachers on the Davis campus of the University of California, finds their views almost the same.

Developed by Miller (1972, pp. 26-27), many students, faculty and administrators will probably agree with this definition of good teaching:

A good teacher personifies enthusiasm for his students, the area of competence, and life itself. He knows his subject, can explain it clearly, and is willing to do so—in or out of class. Class periods are interesting, and at times, alive with excitement. He approaches his area of competence and his students with integrity that is neither stiff nor pompous, and his attitude and demeanor are more caught than taught.

Evaluating Teaching
In general the qualities that are the benchmarks of a good teacher have been repeatedly mentioned in innumerable research studies and position papers. The next question is, how can the presence (or absence) of these qualities in a teacher be known?

Students, faculty colleagues, administrators, and the teachers themselves, all have a part, albeit limited, to play in what is actually a shared determination. This is based on the premise that several sources of information are probably better than one. Students, faculty colleagues, administrators, and the teachers themselves are therefore components of the collective judgment of teaching performance.

Students can, and do, provide reliable and valid appraisals of both the course and the instructor, provided the questions they are asked to answer are appropriate and properly answerable by students, and the rating forms are properly prepared and administered.

The most serious obstacle confronting faculty colleague appraisal of a teacher's performance is the prohibition on many campuses against classroom observation by peers. Thus, direct access to a teacher's classroom performance, an excellent potential source of information, is lost to the evaluative process. In some colleges and universities, where the conditions have slowly and successfully nurtured a reciprocal feeling of trust, respect, and support, classroom observation by peers is accepted as a necessary and constructive part of teacher evaluation. On campuses prohibiting classroom observation, the teacher's colleagues can still form a judgment on performance by careful examination of the course syllabi, classroom handouts, reading and reference lists, examinations, student projects, term papers, and other such clues.

Student learning, as measured by classroom or national tests, has proven useful to some institutions in assessing teaching performance. But the difficulties of present measurements of student learning have prevented its widespread adoption. Two promising approaches to measuring student growth—matrix item sampling and edumetric tests—have recently been developed and may prove valuable.

College and university administrators—department chairmen and academic deans—are an important source of teacher evaluation, even though they rarely venture into the classroom and therefore rely on their own informational sources for judgments on effective teaching.

Teacher self-appraisal, if carefully and honestly performed, can be of inestimable value not only to the accuracy and reliability of the collective judgment of teaching performance, but also as an immediate and effective impetus to improve the teaching performance.

Evaluating Research and Publication

The proper evaluation of research and publication has long been a bone of contention. Some professors advance the argument that research and publication earn the highest esteem and rewards— even more so than classroom teaching itself—only because of the ease with which they can be evaluated. Gustad (1961, p. 206) dissents and argues that "the ease with which research (and publication) is evaluated is more apparent than real." In fact, rather than be accorded a serious and critical appraisal, at many colleges and universities research and publication is merely counted. What enters the numerical tally, however, differs from institution to institution. Some count as bona fide publications only the so-called "refereed" journals and thus relegate to the academic dustbin some excellent non-referred publications. Others count only research-based articles and dismiss theoretical articles no matter how

13

noteworthy. And some tally articles on applied research problems and ignore any article devoted to basic research.

Complicating the matter still further, at many colleges and universities the research and publication is put through different kinds of evaluative wringers. There is committee evaluation, national reputation of the writer, journal quality, reference citation in another publication, and on-campus reputation. Some institutions place high store on the faculty resumé or publications list (referred to in the corridors as the "brag sheet") and on reprints that somehow find their way to the desks of important colleagues and administrators.

In the evaluation of research and publication, in those institutions which have simply not established categories of articles and publications, confusion reigns. The result is that considerable uncertainty operates in the minds of the professors and the faculty committees evaluating them as to just what is and is not important. The elimination of this confusion will be a valued dividend from the establishment of a systematic evaluation program.

The teaching vs. research controversy has served to heat up academe for generations. Unfortunately, all the heat has generated little light.

Some teachers maintain that they cannot be stimulating and up-to-date in their classrooms unless they are personally engaged in research in their favorite areas. Others argue with equal vigor that the kind of research practiced in colleges and universities only indirectly, if at all, is related to classroom teaching.

This knot cannot be unraveled because, unfortunately, there is little reliable evidence on the relationship between teaching and research. It seems likely that debate over whether or not they are complementary activities will continue for generations.

Evaluating Institutional Service and Student Advising

Faculty members are expected to serve on many committees which are concerned with governance, curriculum, discipline, promotion, student affairs, recruitment. It is taken as an article of faith that all faculty members on all committees are operating at high efficiency. So when decisions on tenure, promotion or salary increase are being made, the length of the professor's committee list is automatically translated into the size of his institutional contribution. The longer the list, the greater the contribution. In this alchemy, quantity is transmuted into quality.

Beaird (1975, p.48), after noting the disintegration of excellence that such practices create, argues: "If excellence is the goal, excellence must be recognized and rewarded. If quantity is the goal and is so rewarded, quantity will become the standard."

14

Although most colleges and universities include student advising as an institutional service, it receives only passing attention from many promotion committees. At very few institutions have the necessary criteria been developed for appraising the quality of a professor's contribution as student advisor. This is an unfortunate omission which is easily corrected, and should be.

Chapter 2

Current National Practices— Good and Bad

Some professors believe that the new interest in undergraduate teaching is derivative of the very real difficulty today in achieving professional visibility. First, tight institutional budgets have largely precluded lending a financial helping hand to professors wishing to participate in professional meetings. Second, many scholarly publications are rejecting unsolicited manuscripts at a rate sometimes exceeding 90 percent. As a result, professors have been forced to turn to on-campus activities, including teaching, to remain professionally visible.

As a further consequence, how an institution appraises a faculty member's performance has emerged as a touchy and awesomely important subject since a professional life may depend on it.

To learn just what policies and practices are in actual use by institutions in evaluating faculty performance, the writer conducted a nationwide survey in the Spring of 1978.

Its twofold purpose was (1) to examine critically the wide range of practices, and (2) to suggest which practices are in urgent need of improvement.

Procedure

To assure the widest coverage, the entire population of accredited, 4-year, undergraduate, liberal arts colleges listed in the federal government's *Educational Directory* (1977) was surveyed. Only university-related liberal arts colleges were excluded so as to make the population more manageable.

Of the 807 academic deans receiving the questionnaire, 680 (84.2 percent) replied. This unusually high response suggests perhaps the seriousness with which faculty evaluation is looked upon by the deans.

Table 1 contains the number and percentage of institutions included in the analysis.

16

Table 1.
Number and percentage of institutions
included in the analysis

Type of Institution	Number included	Percentage
Unspecified as Private or Public	10	1.5
Private liberal arts college	567	83.4
Public liberal arts college	103	15.1
Total	680	100

To the completed questionnaires, some deans attached commit-tee reports and sample evaluation forms used at their colleges. Although these discrete documents do not lend themselves to formal analysis, they are noted when appropriate in the discussion of the data.

The questionnaire (see Appendix) used in the study overlapped the forms initially developed by the American Council on Education (1967) and later adapted by the writer (1973) and the Educational Testing Service (1977). It was designed to gain information on institutional policies and practices in evaluating faculty performance in such matters as teaching, research/scholarship, and institutional service, in connection with promotion in rank, salary increase and tenure.

In the questionnaire, each question on overall faculty perform-ance and college service called for a response on a four-point scale: major factor, minor factor, not a factor, not applicable. Each question on the assessment of teaching and scholarship/research required response on a different four-point scale: always used, usually used, seldom used, never used. The average response was computed for both public and private institutions. Where appropri-ate, t-tests were used to investigate response differences.

Findings

The findings are presented in five sections: (1) the factors used in evaluating overall faculty performance; (2) The sources of information in evaluating teaching; (3) The kinds of information used to judge scholarship/research; (4) The factors in the assessment of college service; (5) The personal judgments of academic deans in faculty evaluation.

(1) OVERALL FACULTY PERFORMANCE

When considering a faculty member for promotion in rank, salary increase, or tenure, institutions choose and weigh among many

17

factors. The questionnaire included 13 general criteria in connection with evaluation of overall faculty performance.

In analyzing the responses, numerical weights were assigned so that "major factor" carried a one, "minor factor" a two, and "not a factor" (or "not applicable") a three. This method of summary ratings yields a reasonably accurate picture (Gustad, 1961). Weights for each factor were added, and the sum was divided by the number of responses to yield an arithmetic mean for each. Then, within each category (private or public liberal arts college), factors were ranked in terms of mean scores, a rank of one being assigned to the factor with the lowest mean, a thirteen to the factor with the highest.

This ranking process—which was used by the American Council on Education in an earlier faculty evaluation study—simplifies identification of the most important factors.

Table 2 summarizes the relative importance of factors considered in evaluating overall faculty performance. Both private and public liberal arts colleges reported that classroom teaching was the most important factor in assessing performance. Mean scores are exceedingly low and demonstrate that almost every surveyed college considers teaching a "major factor" in overall faculty evaluation.

Second in importance, are student advising and campus committee work. Clearly, today more than ever, liberal arts colleges are keeping their eyes open to a professor's on-campus activities. They are considered tangible evidence of a professor's contribution to the institution's effort to keep students content and in school.

By contrast, only limited attention is given to some off-campus, formerly traditional, hallmarks of academic success. Such former benchmarks as research, publication, and activity in professional societies, have been demoted by the responding academic deans.

The statistical trends were underlined by comments from many deans. Typically, the dean of a private liberal arts college in Florida wrote: "The ideal professor here is one who devotes himself to teaching and to on-campus committee work." The dean of a private college in Massachusetts said: "Publish or perish is no longer the rule of thumb here." A public liberal arts college dean in Nebraska wrote: "Provided it doesn't interfere with their teaching perform-ance, we like to see our faculty engage in some research and publication. But teaching is given higher priority on our campus."

Private and public liberal arts colleges come to a parting of the ways when it comes to research, publication, and activity in professional societies. Private colleges view these activities as less important than public colleges.

Even more diverse, are the private and public colleges' views on a professor's personal characteristics. Loyalty, compatability, and

Table 2.
Factors Considered in Evaluating
Overall Faculty Performance in
Liberal Arts Colleges

Factors	Private College (N=567)		Public College (N=103)		Total (N=680)[*]	
	Mean	Rank	Mean	Rank	Mean	Rank
Classroom teaching	1.01	1	1.00	1	1.01	1
Supervision of graduate study	2.28	10	2.25	11	2.26	10
Supervision of honors program	2.34	11	2.47	13	2.36	11
Research	1.86	6	1.70	4	1.83	6
Publication	1.92	8	1.76	5	1.89	8
Public service	1.99	9	1.78	7	1.96	9
Consultation (gov't. business)	2.41	12	2.39	12	2.41	12
Activity in professional soc.	1.89	7	1.81	8	1.88	7
Student advising	1.32	2	1.46	2	1.34	2
Campus committee work	1.51	3	1.64	3	1.52	3
Length of service in rank	1.54	4	1.77	6	1.57	4
Competing job offers	2.67	13	2.84	14	2.69	13
Personal attributes	1.68	5	2.05	10	1.74	5
Total mean	1.88		1.92		1.88	

[*]includes 10 colleges not specified as private or public.

religious activity are given high marks in private institutions. It should be noted, however, that these private institutions tend to be smaller, less affluent, than the public institutions and (see Table 2) tend to measure loyalty by the duration of professorial service.

Near the bottom of the list are such items as supervision of graduate study, supervision of honors programs, consultation, and competing job offers as factors in the overall evaluation of faculty.

Total means were computed to determine the number of factors rated toward the low end. If an institution rated only one or two factors low, they would have a higher total mean than an institution rating several factors low. The difference between total means for private and public liberal arts colleges is very small, suggesting that both institutions consider a wide range of factors in assessing overall faculty performance.

The academic deans' views on whether an item is a "major factor" or "not a factor" are reported in Table 3. The table contains several surprises. There are differences not only between the private and public liberal arts colleges but also within each group. For example, 22.9 percent of the private college deans viewed research as a "major factor" whereas 9.5 percent viewed research as "not a factor." Similarly, 23.3 percent of the public college deans reported personal attributes as a "major factor" whereas 28.2 percent reported personal attributes as "not a factor."

Table 3.
Frequency of Use of Factors Considered in
Evaluating Overall Faculty Performance in
Liberal Arts Colleges

Factors	Private Colleges (N=567)		Public Colleges (N=103)	
	major factor	not a factor	major factor	not a factor
	(%)	(%)	(%)	(%)
Classroom teaching	98.6	0.0	100.0	0.0
Supervision of graduate study	1.8	6.5	4.9	20.4
Supervision of honors program	2.3	15.3	3.9	30.1
Research	22.9	9.5	33.0	3.9
Publication	17.3	9.3	28.2	4.9
Public Service	10.9	10.4	29.1	6.8
Consultation (gov't. business)	1.1	36.0	1.9	39.8
Activity in professional societies	16.6	6.2	19.4	1.0
Student advising	68.8	1.9	55.3	1.9
Campus committee work	51.0	2.3	36.9	1.0
Length of service in rank	52.9	8.1	33.0	10.7
Competing job offers	3.4	61.2	1.9	73.8
Personal attributes	41.4	10.9	23.3	28.2

In liberal arts colleges, classroom teaching is the easy front runner as a measure of faculty performance. Far behind, by 30 percentage points, in second place, is student advising. Worthy of mention, however, is that although classroom teaching holds undisputed first place in professorial appraisal in private liberal arts colleges, many academic deans of both institutions consider other activities also of major importance. For example, eight other activities are marked "major factor" by at least 19 percent of the public institution deans, and six such activities were so qualified by the same or greater percentage of private institution deans.

Lastly, the public colleges tend to rely more on research, publications, public service, and professional society activity, and the private colleges tend to emphasize campus committee work, length of service in rank, and personal attributes.

20

Several years ago, the writer reported the results of a survey on evaluative policies on faculty performance by private colleges (see Seldin, 1975). The report concluded with the unhappy finding that meaningful evaluation was rare because the methods employed were frequently inaccurate and unreliable. Since 1973, some institutions have been accredited, a few closed and others merged. But, for the purpose of identifying significant changes and trends in evaluating overall faculty performance, enough overlap exists to warrant comparisons. (Similar base data for public colleges are unfortunately unavailable.)

Table 4 shows how academic deans in private colleges viewed "major factors" in faculty evaluations in 1973 and 1978.

Table 4.
Private Liberal Arts Colleges Citing
"Major Factors" in Evaluating Overall Faculty Performance

Factors	1973 (N=410)	1978 (N=567)
	%	%
Classroom teaching	99.3	98.6
Supervision of graduate study	1.9	1.8
Supervision of honors program	2.9	2.3
Research	22.2	22.9
Publication	17.1	17.3
Public Service	12.9	10.9
Consultation (gov't. business)	0.7	1.1
Activity in professional societies	15.8	16.6
Student advising	68.8	68.8
Campus committee work	49.5	51.0
Length of service in rank	54.4	52.9
Competing job offers	3.2	3.4
Personal attributes	53.2	41.1

Even a cursory examination of this table reveals that things have not changed very much. In fact, of the thirteen factors only one—personal attributes—changed by 3 percent or more. Similar stability also turns up in the data in Table 5, which reports t-tests of differences in mean scores of factors considered in overall evaluations. The data indicate significant difference at the .05 level between the mean scores of only two factors in 1973 and 1978. These two factors are competing job offers and personal attributes.

The mean scores were calculated by adding the assigned numerical weights for each factor (as previously described) and then dividing the sum by the number of responses to yield for each an arithmetic mean.

The near unanimity of the 1973 and 1978 mean scores suggests that despite the persistent financial duress in which private colleges

21

Table 5.
T-Tests of Differences in Mean Scores of Factors
Considered in Private Liberal Arts Colleges in
Evaluating Overall Faculty Performance

Factors	1973 (N=410) mean score	1978 (N=567) mean score	t
Classroom teaching	1.01	1.01	-0.26
Supervision of graduate study	2.17	2.28	-0.96
Supervision of honors program	2.34	2.34	0.15
Research	1.90	1.96	1.04
Publication	1.93	1.92	0.50
Public service	2.01	1.99	0.40
Consultation (gov't. business)	2.47	2.41	1.65
Activity in professional societies	1.93	1.89	1.16
Student advising	1.34	1.32	0.59
Campus committee work	1.51	1.51	0.17
Length of service in rank	1.48	1.54	-1.26
Competing job offers	2.58	2.67	-2.17°
Personal attributes	1.51	1.68	-4.05°

The test used was a t-test for differences in independent proportions.
°significant at .05 level of confidence

operate, no real change has resulted in evaluation of *overall* performance.

Drastic change has been reserved, however, for evaluations of faculty *teaching* performance.

(2) EVALUATING TEACHING PERFORMANCE

Since classroom teaching was cited overwhelmingly as the single most important factor in faculty evaluation by almost all liberal arts colleges, it is of special pertinence to examine the sources of information on which such an important judgment was based.

Table 6 summarizes the relative importance of 15 sources of information used in the evaluative process.

Most frequently cited are the evaluations by deans and chairmen, leaving as the crucial question how their evaluations are constructed.

Deans and chairmen have easy, personal access to a professor's schedule and enrollment load, but unless they also visit the classroom they are forced to rely on other information sources to provide the basis for their administrative judgments.

As denoted in Table 6, systematic student ratings and colleagues' opinions score highly as sources of information in both private and public institutions. But whereas private colleges accord alumni opinions far greater importance, perhaps the result of traditionally stronger alumni associations, the public colleges bestow such

22

Table 6.
Sources of Information Considered in Evaluating
Faculty Teaching Performance in Liberal Arts Colleges

Sources of Information	Private Colleges (N=567)		Public Colleges (N=103)		Total (N=680)*	
	Mean	Rank	Mean	Rank	Mean	Rank
Systematic student ratings	1.66	3	1.50	3	1.64	3
Informal student opinions	2.26	7	2.64	10	2.31	7
Classroom visits	2.76	10	2.17	7	2.67	10
Colleagues' opinions	1.73	4	1.69	4	1.73	4
Scholarly research and publication	2.36	8	2.21	8	2.34	8
Student examination performance	3.04	13	3.32	12	3.08	13
Chairman evaluation	1.27	1	1.20	1	1.27	1
Dean evaluation	1.30	2	1.40	2	1.32	2
Course syllabi and examinations	2.40	9	2.52	9	2.41	9
Long term follow-up students	3.15	15	3.28	11	3.16	15
Enrollment in elective courses	2.98	11	3.34	13	3.04	11
Alumni opinions	2.99	12	3.39	15	3.06	12
Committee evaluation	2.08	6	1.90	5	2.06	5
Grade distributions	3.07	14	3.35	14	3.12	14
Self-evaluation or report	2.07	5	2.08	6	2.08	6
Total mean	2.34		2.40		2.35	

*includes 10 colleges not specified as private or public

importance on classroom visits, perhaps as a response to pressure for accountability by state legislatures. Far down the scale of importance, both private and public colleges, are student examination performance, long-term follow-up students, and grade distribution.

Table 7 shows the distribution of dean response to each source of information as "always used" or "never used." Differences appear. For example, private college deans give greater weight than public college deans to systematic student ratings, classroom visits, scholarly research and publication. Furthermore, although chairman and dean evaluations are unsurpassed as sources of information in private and public colleges, in the latter the chairman's evaluation was appreciatively more important than the dean's.

Surprisingly, private and public colleges report considerable internal variation. For example, self-evaluation is cited as "always used" by approximately 36 percent of the private and public colleges. But almost 11 percent of the private, and 14 percent of the

23

public colleges, cited self-evaluation as "never used." Similarly, although 45.1 percent of the private colleges reported committee evaluation is "always used," some 17.3 percent reported it is "never used." And although scholarly research and publication was cited by 27.2 percent of the public colleges as "always used," some 12.6 percent reported it is "never used."

It is clear that private and public colleges lack a uniform approach to the sources of information on which teaching competency is based.

Table 7.
Frequency of Use of Sources of Information Considered
In Evaluating Teaching Performance in
Liberal Arts Colleges

Sources of Information	Private Colleges (N=567)		Public Colleges (N=103)	
	always used	never used	always used	never used
	%	%	%	%
Systematic student ratings	53.1	2.8	64.1	4.9
Informal student opinion	16.9	4.9	5.8	10.7
Classroom visits	11.1	15.0	32.0	6.8
Colleagues' opinions	42.0	1.2	46.6	2.9
Scholarly research and publication	18.5	10.2	27.2	12.6
Student examination performance	3.2	25.9	8.7	39.8
Chairman evaluation	79.9	3.0	82.5	1.0
Dean evaluation	77.4	1.9	73.8	3.9
Course syllabi and examinations	14.3	9.2	11.7	12.6
Long term follow-up students	2.6	30.5	0.0	35.9
Enrollment in elective courses	2.8	26.5	1.9	45.6
Alumni opinions	3.9	23.6	1.0	47.6
Committee evaluation	45.1	17.3	54.4	15.5
Grade distributions	2.5	28.9	0.0	45.6
Self-evaluation or report	36.3	10.8	37.9	13.6

Table 8 shows the frequency with which private college deans cite a source of information as "always used," and compares this frequency with the 1973 study. Several substantial changes turn up. The information gathering process has broadened over the years, tending to become more structured and systematized, and suggests that many institutions are receptive to ways of strengthening their evaluative procedures.

All this can be gleaned not only from the tabular percentages but also from the frequent comments by deans. For example, a New

York dean wrote: "Students, faculty peers, and the professor himself, all provide input now to our assessment process." A Texas dean said: "We are in the process of completely revamping an evaluation system which has been very unsystematic. More sources of input will be used and the data will be more carefully compiled."

As previously noted, chairman and dean evaluations are the runaway leaders as the sources of information cited as "always used." But that leadership now shows clear signs of slippage as both sources drop several percentage points in importance.

Evaluation by committee continues its stellar role in faculty assessment and even has added a few percentage points in importance.

How do administrators and faculty arrive at their judgments? How solid is their information?

There is compelling evidence to indicate that these judgments are given formative shape by reliance on student ratings. The use of these student ratings has expanded rapidly in recent years and today, for perhaps the first time, student ratings influence personnel decisions at a majority of liberal arts colleges. Their rapid growth has also exacerbated the conflict over their value. A Georgia dean regards student ratings as, "The most onerous factor in higher

Table 8.
Private Liberal Arts Colleges Citing
Sources of Information as Always Used
in Evaluating Teaching Performance

Sources of Information	1973 (N=410)	1978 (N=567)
	%	%
Systematic student ratings	29.1	53.1
Informal student opinion	17.8	16.9
Classroom visits	4.9	11.1
Colleagues' opinions	39.6	42.0
Scholarly research and publication	19.3	18.5
Student examination performance	3.7	3.2
Chairman evaluation	85.3	79.9
Dean evaluation	85.3	77.4
Course syllabi and examinations	10.5	14.3
Long term follow-up students	2.2	2.6
Enrollment in elective courses	2.9	2.8
Alumni opinions	2.0	3.9
Committee evaluation	42.3	45.1
Grade distribution	2.4	2.5
Self-evaluation or report	19.8	36.3

education today. I'll quit as dean before I'll allow it here." Equally typical, on the other side of the argument, is the Oregon dean who insists, "If I must trust only one source of data on teaching, I trust the students. I have found student views to be objective, thoughtful and fair."

Classroom visits, despite more than a two-fold increase, are part of the evaluative process in a negligible number of liberal arts colleges. In general, professors are not receptive to classroom visits, which are considered demeaning of professional standing, and resistance, articulate and sometimes bitter, has curtailed their use. On this issue, academic deans find themselves divided. A Pennsylvania dean argued: "Classroom visits are essential to the evaluation process. It's the only way to really know what's going on behind the closed door." A Nebraska dean observed: "When the professor knows he's being watched by someone whose opinion will determine his tenure or promotion, his performance may depend more on his nerve than on his teaching skill." If classroom visits are to achieve their potential as a primary source of information, they will first have to achieve an unblemished reputation for objectivity and fairness.

Self-evaluation is now considered by more than one-third of the deans as a source of information which is "always used." This is almost double the figure cited in 1973, a dramatic rise. It suggests more recognition by private colleges that their faculty members should be an integral part of a multi-source information system on teaching performance.

However, self-evaluation is still a subject for controversy. To a Vermont dean, "Self-evaluation . . . is the cornerstone of our faculty appraisal system." To a Kansas dean, self-evaluation is self-serving: "I cannot believe that a professor would detail his teaching faults, knowing his contract renewal, promotion in rank, and tenure hang in the balance."

In recent years, private colleges have partly dismantled and reconstructed their procedures for assessing the teaching (as distinct from the overall) performance of their faculty. Of the fifteen sources of information listed in the 1973 and 1978 surveys, five moved up or down by 5 or more percent. These are student ratings, classroom visits, chairman evaluation, dean evaluation, and self-evaluation. Two sources of information, student ratings and self-evaluation, each jumped in use by more than 15 percent.

This shift of position is also indicated in the t-tests of differences in mean scores of sources of information considered in evaluating teaching performance, as reported in Table 9. An analysis indicates significant differences at the .01 level between the mean scores of seven sources of information in the 1973 and 1978 surveys. The seven are: student ratings, informal student opinion, classroom visits, dean evaluation, course syllabi and examinations, enrollment in elective courses, and self-evaluation. Significant difference at the .05 level is found between the mean scores of one source of information in 1973 and 1978—alumni opinions.

Table 9.
T-Tests of Differences in Mean Scores of Sources of Information
Considered in Private Liberal Arts Colleges
In Evaluating Teaching Performance

Sources of information	1973 (N=410)	1978 (N=567)	t
	Mean score	Mean score	
Systematic student ratings	2.20	1.66	9.48°°
Informal student opinion	2.04	2.26	-4.34°°
Classroom visits	2.98	2.76	4.12°°
Colleagues' opinions	1.76	1.73	0.46
Scholarly research and publication	2.30	2.36	-1.06
Student examination performance	2.95	3.04	-1.89
Chairman evaluation	1.22	1.27	-1.33
Dean evaluation	1.19	1.30	-2.89°°
Course syllabi and examinations	2.56	2.40	3.06°°
Long term follow-up students	3.13	3.15	-0.39
Enrollment in elective courses	2.79	2.98	-3.85°°
Alumni opinions	3.09	2.99	2.07°
Committee evaluation	2.17	2.08	1.15
Grade distribution	3.05	3.07	-0.38
Self-evaluation or report	2.58	2.07	7.48°°

The test was a t-test for differences in independent proportions.
°significant at .05 level of confidence
°°significant at .01 level of confidence

Table 10 shows the percentage of liberal arts colleges using and/or conducting research on rating forms. About two-thirds of the colleges acknowledged using rating forms, which were filled in

Table 10.
Frequency of Use and Research on Rating Forms
to Evaluate Faculty Teaching Performance in
Liberal Arts Colleges

	Private Colleges (N=567) %		Public Colleges (N=103) %		Total (N=680)°° %	
	yes	no	yes	no	yes	no
Use of rating forms	62.1°	33.5	68.9	27.2	62.8	32.9
Research on rating forms	10.1	80.6	9.7	79.6	10.0	80.1

°"yes" and "no" percentages do not add to 100% as some institutions failed to answer this question.
°°includes 10 colleges not specified as private or public.

by students, faculty colleagues, or administrators. Surprising and disheartening, however, was the minimal study reported by the colleges on the validity or utility of the rating forms. It explains why masses of faculty members and even some administrators lack confidence in the instruments they use.

(3) EVALUATING SCHOLARSHIP/RESEARCH

Table 11 summarizes the deans' considerations in evaluating faculty scholarship/research. From the data it is clear that public and private colleges hold wide differences in both the importance and quality assessment of scholarship/research. The much lower total mean scores indicate that public colleges hold research and publication in higher esteem than private colleges. This esteem is probably generated in part by the need of the public colleges to display voluminous evidence of important faculty scholarship and publication, so as to warrant continued public funding by state legislatures.

In assessing the quality of scholarship/research, the public colleges apply three major yardsticks: books written by the professor as the sole or senior author, monographs or book chapters, and books written as the junior author or as editor. The quality of the work is judged more meritorious if it wins honors or awards from a professional organization.

Private colleges also place high store in books written entirely by the professor, or by the professor as senior author. But private colleges give almost equal importance to papers read at professional meetings and to articles in professional journals. The quality of the work is most frequently judged by department chairmen and deans. But the high total mean scores, in absolute terms, indicate that private liberal arts colleges are inclined to consider other areas of faculty performance as more weighty than scholarship/research.

This conclusion is supported by the following typical comments from private college deans:

"We are primarily a teaching college and use scholarship/research performance on a limited basis, if at all."—an Iowa dean.

"We emphasize excellent teaching; research and publication are not mandatory."—a California dean.

"Teaching performance is most important . . . put research and publication a distinct second."—a Massachusetts dean.

"We require no publication or research."—a Florida dean.

"We consider above all if the faculty member is a good teacher. Everything else is secondary."—a Kansas dean.

"Teaching, advising, and committee work are the principal items

28

Table 11.
Information Considered in Evaluating Scholarship/Research Performance in Liberal Arts Colleges

Types of information	Private Colleges (N=567)		Public Colleges (N=103)		Total Colleges (N=680)**	
	mean	rank	mean	rank	mean	rank
Publication in all professional journals	1.83	3	1.57	5	1.79	2
Articles in *quality* journals	1.89	5	1.54	4	1.84	5
Unpublished papers or reports	2.47	7	2.45	7	2.47	7
Papers at professional meetings	1.82	1*	1.58	6	1.79	2
Citations to published materials	2.72	8	2.47	8	2.68	8
Books as sole or senior author	1.82	1*	1.39	1	1.76	1
Books as junior author or editor	1.91	6	1.52	3	1.86	6
Monographs or chapters in books	1.85	4	1.47	2	1.80	4
Total mean	2.04		1.75		2.00	

*tie in rank

Quality of research and publication as judged by:						
Peers at the institution	1.94	3	1.87	4	1.93	3
Peers at other institutions	2.83	8	2.89	8	2.84	8
Department chairman	1.81	1	1.69	2	1.79	1
Dean	1.92	2	1.86	3	1.91	2
Self-evaluations	2.55	6	2.33	7	2.51	6
Grants or funding received	2.40	5	2.13	5	2.37	5
Referee or editor of professional journal	2.76	7	2.27	6	2.69	7
Honors or awards from profession	1.99	4	1.65	1	1.94	4
Total mean	2.28		2.09		2.25	

**includes 10 colleges not specified as private or public.

of concern. Research and writing is considered in a minor way as evidence of professional involvement."—a Texas dean.

Table 12 shows the considerations which are "always used" or "never used" by the deans in evaluating scholarship/research. As noted, books written as the sole or senior author predominate as a consideration in both public and private colleges. Department chairmen are the standard judges of quality. Unpublished articles and monographs, references in publications, and judgments by faculty members in other colleges, fall into the lightweight class as considerations of scholarship/research.

In general, despite an overlap, a wide chasm exists between public and private colleges in judging scholarship/research. Consistently, with only one exception (unpublished papers or reports), public colleges come up with a higher percentage in the "always used" column of 16 considerations than the private colleges. In the case of "books as sole or senior author," the gap is almost 30 percentage points.

There is also wide fluctuation within both public and private colleges. For example, 19 percent of the private colleges report they "always used" self-evaluations, whereas 20.3 percent report never using them. Similarly, 28.2 percent of the public colleges report grants or outside funding as "always used" in considering scholarship/research, but 12.6 percent say this consideration is "never used."

Table 12.
Frequency of Use of Information Considered in
Evaluating Scholarship/Research Performance in
Liberal Arts Colleges

Types of Information	Private College (N=567)		Public College (N=103)	
	always used	never used	always used	never used
	%	%	%	%
Publication in all professional journals	45.0	6.3	51.5	2.9
Articles in *quality* journals	42.5	7.4	55.3	2.9
Unpublished papers or reports	14.3	10.9	10.7	7.8
Papers at professional meetings	39.9	5.6	52.4	1.9
Citations to published materials	13.8	21.2	15.5	11.7
Books as sole or senior author	50.1	8.5	69.9	2.9
Books as junior author or editor	44.6	8.5	58.3	2.9
Monographs or chapters in books	45.5	8.1	60.2	1.9
Quality of research and publication as judged by:				
Peers at the institution	42.3	12.3	43.7	8.7
Peers at other institutions	11.3	27.2	12.6	28.2
Department chairman	47.4	10.4	50.5	6.8
Dean	40.0	9.3	42.7	7.8
Self-evaluations	19.0	20.3	23.3	16.5
Grants or funding received	21.9	17.1	28.2	12.6
Referee or editor of professional journal	16.9	28.6	33.0	16.5
Honors or awards from professional	36.9	11.3	47.6	4.9

(4) EVALUATING COLLEGE SERVICE

Table 13 summarizes the deans' evaluative views on the faculty's service to the college. In this instance, public and private colleges are in general agreement on the important components of this service. The ranking of factors by public and private colleges is almost uniform, with eight of the nine factors within a range of one rank.

Total mean scores for public and private colleges are close, 1.71 and 1.78 which indicates a similar weighting of factors. For example, the foremost two factors to the deans of private colleges, academic advising and serving on college-wide committees, are also foremost to the deans of public colleges, even though the sequence is reversed. Mean scores for both colleges are exceptionally low, indicating the critical importance to both of academic advising and service on college-wide committees.

Typical comments by the deans tend to support the statistical

Table 13.
Factors Considered in Evaluating College Service
Performance in Liberal Arts Colleges

Factors	Private College (N=567)		Public College (N=103)		Total (N=680)°°	
	mean	rank	mean	rank	mean	rank
Service on department committee	1.55	3	1.45	3	1.54	3
Service on college-wide committee	1.20	2	1.22	1	1.20	1°
Academic advising	1.17	1	1.32	2	1.20	1°
Non-academic student counseling	1.86	5	2.22	9	1.92	6
Willingness to teach undesirable courses	2.04	8	2.09	7	2.04	8
Advisor to student organizations	1.89	6	1.91	5	1.89	5
Service as student recruiter	2.15	9	2.19	8	2.16	9
Departmental administrative duties	1.61	4	1.64	4	1.62	4
Participation in campus symposia	1.91	7	1.99	6	1.93	7
Total mean	1.71		1.78		1.72	

°tie in rank
°°includes 10 colleges not specified as private or public

31

data. "In evaluating faculty performance, we place a premium on service on college-wide committees," wrote a Pennsylvania dean. "Skill in academic advising is nearly as important here as skill in the classroom," said an Arizona dean. "Academic advising and service on college-wide committees," wrote an Oregon dean, "are given more weight in tenure and promotion decisions than research and publication."

Table 14 shows how deans view each component of college service as a "major factor" or "not a factor." In general, the four predominant "major factors" are academic advising, service on college-wide committees, departmental administrative duties, and service on department committees. The hefty importance of these four areas of college service is also indicated, conversely, by the slender percentage of colleges reporting them as "not a factor."

Although private colleges emphasize academic advising, they grant almost equal weight to service on college-wide committees. For public colleges, service on college-wide committees is the front runner in importance, with academic advising and service on departmental committees considered "major factors," but trailing.

Table 14.
Frequency of Use of Factors Considered in
Evaluating College Service in Liberal Arts Colleges

Factors	Private College (N=567)		Public College (N=103)	
	major factor	not a factor	major factor	not a factor
	%	%	%	%
Service on department committee	43.4	2.3	54.4	1.0
Service on college-wide committee	80.2	0.9	76.7	0.0
Academic advising	82.2	0.7	66.0	1.0
Non-academic student counseling	25.0	12.2	10.7	31.1
Willingness to teach undesirable courses	20.6	23.8	17.5	25.2
Advisor to student organizations	21.9	10.9	18.4	9.7
Service as student recruiter	11.8	25.6	10.7	27.2
Departmental administrative duties	44.4	6.9	40.8	6.8
Participation in campus symposia	22.0	13.8	14.6	13.6

Non-academic student counseling is accorded less importance than academic advising by both private and public colleges. And both give least importance to student recruiting service.

(5) PERSONAL JUDGMENTS OF ACADEMIC DEANS

Table 15 denotes the personal judgments of the deans, which turn out to be similar in private and public colleges. On none of the six questionnaire items does the response by private and public college

Table 15.
Percentage of Response by Academic Deans of
Liberal Arts Colleges to Personal Judgment Questions.

Questionnaire items	Private College (N=567)		Public College (N=103)	
	agree°	disagree	agree	disagree
	%°°	%	%	%
1. The results of systematic student evaluation of a faculty member's teaching performance indicate more about a teacher's popularity than about his teaching performance.	33.9	66.1	43.7	54.3
2. The results of systematic student evaluation of a faculty member's teaching performance should be made public.	23.4	76.2	33.0	66.0
3. Systematic and planned classroom visitation by faculty colleagues for the purpose of evaluating a faculty member's teaching performance is an invasion of academic privacy.	15.2	84.1	8.7	91.3
4. Results of an institutionalized uniform approach to faculty self-evaluation should be one of the important components in evaluation of faculty teaching performance.	86.3	12.7	84.4	13.6
5. The academic personnel policies and practices used to evaluate a faculty member's teaching performance are well known by most members of the faculty.	85.5	14.1	86.4	11.6
6. Academic personnel decisions made in liberal arts colleges are based primarily on objective information (that is, information that is rational, impersonal and unprejudiced).	51.1	45.8	57.3	38.9

°Agree and strongly agree categories in questionnaire are combined in this Table as are categories disagree and strongly disagree.
°°Percentages do not total 100 percent as some survey respondents omitted this question.

deans vary by more than 12 percent. For example, 85.5 percent of the private college deans and 86.4 of the public college deans agreed with the questionnaire item: "The academic personnel policies and practices used to evaluate a faculty member's teaching performance are well known by most members of the faculty." Similarly, 86.3 percent of one and 84.4 percent of the other agreed with the questionnaire item: "Results of an institutionalized uniform approach to faculty self-evaluation should be one of the important components in evaluation of faculty teaching performance."

Of course, in either group, private or public, there were splits in personal opinions. For example, private college deans split almost down the middle on the questionnaire item, "Academic personnel decisions...are based primarily on objective information...." Public college deans were almost equally divided on the item, "The results of systematic student evaluation of a faculty member's teaching performance indicate more about a teacher's popularity than about his teaching performance."

Conclusion

Classroom teaching is the most important factor in evaluating faculty performance in public and private liberal arts colleges. Student advising and campus committee work follow in importance.

With today's tightened budgets, these colleges are paying closer attention to the faculty's on-campus activities. This is in sharp contrast to the hallmarks of academic success formerly in vogue. Today, research, publication, activity in professional societies, although they still count, have somewhat deflated importance.

The question that still nags for an answer, however, is whether classroom teaching in truth carries as much clout in promotion and tenure decisions as the deans report. How much lip service is being paid by the deans? Also questionable is whether the faculty goes along with the deans on what is important in promotion and tenure decisions.

The study also produces probable evidence that the policies and practices used to evaluate teaching performance are becoming more structured and systematized. Chairman and dean evaluations, while still very important, are losing ground to formal faculty committees, self-evaluation, and colleagues' opinions. And systematic student ratings, for perhaps the first time, are now an integral part in personnel decisions at a majority of liberal arts colleges.

The trend to decentralization and the sharing of decision-making seems clear, as does the growing effort toward the reliability of the evaluative process.

From their responses to the personal judgment questions, it

appears that the academic deans are not troubled by an apparent loss of authority, but instead welcome the changes in the evaluative process. For example, 86 percent of the private college deans and 84 percent of the public college deans report strong personal support for faculty self-evaluation.

Sharp differences turn up in the performance and quality of scholarship/research between the public and private colleges. The public colleges emphasize research and publication and tend to measure faculty productivity by a head-count of books, monographs, and articles in quality journals. Quality is also determined by honors and professional awards. The private colleges, on the contrary, add up the books, papers delivered at professional meetings, and publication in any professional journal, and generally leave quality to the department chairmen and deans.

In college service, the study suggests that private and public colleges are in close agreement. In both colleges, academic advising and service on college-wide and departmental committees are considered primary.

Lastly, it is important to note that, after classroom teaching, student advising and campus committee work now rank second and third in the overall assessment of faculty performance. College service as a factor has thus achieved new eminence.

Chapter 3

Student Evaluation

It is manifestly true that the only direct, daily observers of a professor's classroom teaching performance are the students in the classroom. Students are thus a potentially valuable source of judgmental information in the overall evaluation of a professor. But student judgments and insights are not limited to the classroom. The professor is also judged by his role as academic advisor and by his periodic non-classroom meetings, formal and informal, with the students.

The harvesting of student opinion about a professor can theoretically include an exit interview, a suggestion box, small discussion group, questionnaire to alumni, face-to-face discussion, student testimonial. In practice, a written questionnaire or rating scale generally serves as the predominant, if not only, source of administrative information. In recent years it has become as commonplace in colleges and universities for students to grade professors as for professors to grade students. Today, for perhaps the first time, student evaluations are an accepted component in personnel decisions at a majority of colleges and universities.

It is obvious that the explosive growth of student ratings is directly attributable to the campus unrest in the 1960's. Historically, however, the origins can be traced to the Middle Ages. Then, for instance, at the University of Padua, in Italy, students hired and fired their own teachers. And it was common at the great universities in Paris, Bologna, and Heidelberg for students to express appreciation of a professor by pressing coins into his hand or dropping them into the hood of his gown.

In the United States, student evaluation was born at Harvard in 1924 with the student publication of a *Confidential Guide to Courses*, which offered student appraisal of courses and professors. The publication reportedly is still thriving. Also in the early twenties, the students at the University of Washington filled out the first questionnaires about their professors and today—40,000 questionnaires later—they are still evaluating their professors. It has the distinction of being the oldest ongoing student appraisal program in the nation.

Students have conspicuous assets as judges of teaching which, according to many academics, more than outweigh their youthful inexperience.

Using Student Ratings to Improve Instruction

Does the use of student ratings automatically result in improved teaching? The evidence is mixed. Miller (1971) studied 36 teaching assistants in three courses for college freshmen. Some of them were provided student ratings of their classroom performance during the fifth week into the semester, others were not. Miller found that final semester ratings for both groups of teaching assistants, with and without benefit of mid-semester ratings, lacked significant difference. Conclusion: instruction did not automatically improve after the student ratings.

Similarly, Centra (1972), in a five-college study, found no significant change in final semester ratings from the mid-semester ratings of 400 teachers. But Centra reported that student feedback improved instruction for teachers who had rated themselves more generously than their students. The apparent principle was, the wider the gulf, the more likely the change.

Other researchers report a positive relationship between student ratings and teaching improvement. An early study by Wilson (1932) concluded that teachers who tried to strengthen their weak teaching points, as identified by students, were up-rated five months later by another group of students. More recently, Gage (1972) reported improved classroom instruction when student ratings were accompanied by a theoretical rating of an "ideal" teacher. It suggested that the greater the demonstrated difference between the actual and the ideal teacher, the greater the likelihood of change. Pambookian (1972) confirmed this view by finding that teachers who rated themselves higher than their students improved, whereas teachers whose self-ratings were on a par or lower than the student ratings did not.

In two studies at the University of Michigan, McKeachie (1975, p. 74) found that student ratings led to teaching improvement, but he also found that the improvement was contingent on specific influences. First, it depended on whether the ratings turned up an appraisal which was new to the teacher. Second, it depended on whether the teacher was motivated to improve. Third, it depended also on whether the teacher knew how to go about improving.

It seems clear that student ratings will more likely produce a salutary effect when discussed with the teacher by a sympathetic, knowledgeable colleague who can reassure the teacher that his problems are not unusual or insurmountable and offers appropriate counsel on means of improving his teaching.

On balance, however, enough hard evidence is lacking to prove that student evaluations automatically improve classroom teaching. At most, it is safe to say that student ratings tend to focus attention on possible teaching deficiencies. As Eble (1972, p. 69) suggested, "The ratings themselves may be less important than the discussions they provoke, the power they have to make teaching a live issue on campus, and the favorable effects they may have on the general climate for learning."

Using Student Ratings for Personnel Decisions

Today, due to mounting public interest in teacher accountability, attempts are being made to mandate student ratings as one measure of teacher effectiveness. The controversy over this issue has probably been unnecessarily embittered by the not infrequent abuse of student ratings when making tenure or promotion in rank decisions. There should be no doubt any longer that students are an important factor in teaching evaluation. But their importance depends in large measure on whether they are asked the right questions. As Miller (1975, pp. 31-32) pointed out. "Students are in the best position to judge whether course objectives are clear and the course is well organized, whether the instructor explains clearly, allows for dissent, is patient, is interested in students and how he compares with other instructors with whom they have taken courses."

But students cannot and should not be expected to pass judgment on the currency of course material, the professor's mastery of the subject, the appropriateness of instructional objectives, reading lists or textbooks. These judgments require professional background and should be left to the professor's colleagues.

Thus, student ratings as a source of information about teaching are necessary but not sufficient. Additional information from other sources, carefully weighed, is required if the final judgment is to be sound. This is especially true when evaluating performance for personnel decisions.

How should student ratings be reported to administrators? Reporting the mean ratings of all faculty members in a department or institution simplifies the task for administrators to compute norms, such as percentiles. But prudent administrators will avoid this simplified approach. Faculty members in different courses should be compared on overall ratings instead of ratings on specific behaviors. Thereby, administrators can avoid the difficulty inherent in non-teaching factors, such as class size, which may contribute to variance in class ratings.

In student ratings, probably no more than four or five questions are needed. But they must be validly phrased for all courses, no matter what subject, instructional style or class size. One question can determine how students rate an instructor: excellent, good, fair or poor. McKeachie (1978, p. 271) suggests knowing how much the course "stimulated interest or curiosity" as a further index.

When using student ratings for personnel decisions, it is essential that the forms be administered, collected and tallied systematically. And ratings in several courses and over several semesters are needed to assure a reasonably accurate assessment of a professor by his students.

How do faculty members view the use of student ratings in tenure and promotion decisions? Although few studies have explored this question, McMartin and Rich (1976) report that faculty members are in general agreement that such data have a legitimate place in tenure and promotion decisions, a finding in accord with that obtained by Marsh and Kesler (1976).

Using Student Ratings to Help Students Select a Course and Instructor

Handbooks that report student ratings of courses and instructors are commonplace on the college and university campus. Generally, these ratings are compiled each semester and serve students in their selection of course and instructor. As "consumers," students want more information about a course than a thumbnail description of its content. They want to know how class time is spent, the instructional materials, evaluation procedures, grading standards, frequency and nature of tests and assignments, and the instructional objectives. They want to know also the instructor's reputation for helpfulness, accessibility, sensitivity to student needs, ability to stimulate interest, his clarity, openness to opposing opinions, enthusiasm, classroom preparation, and personal idiosyncrasies.

Conversely, this wealth of information can be useful also to the instructor as the basis for change. Menges (1973) describes this information as reporting rather than evaluating, as the least sensitive yet often the most helpful guide in an overall assessment program. There is practically no faculty opposition to student ratings used as student guidance to course and instructor selection.

Reliability of Student Ratings

The test of reliability is to yield the same result no matter how often or where the test is performed. A reliable instrument of measurement needs to show internal stability and timeless consistency. On student ratings, almost every study measuring their

39

reliability has reported a high level of both correlation in time and internal stability.

Stability. Student ratings once obtained tend to correlate highly with those obtained later on. Guthrie (1954) reported test-retest correlations of .87 and .89 in student ratings of their instructors one year apart. Lovell and Haner (1955) found a .89 correlation between ratings taken two weeks apart. Remmers (1959) reported reliability scores approaching .90 in his research with the widely-used Purdue Rating Scale. More recently, Costin (1968) obtained correlations from .70 to .87 in ratings taken mid-semester and end-of-semester on four instructor probes (skill, feedback, rapport, and structure). Finally, Murray (1973) reported test-retest reliabilities as high as .81 within a class and year.

Consistency. Many researchers have found that questions on student rating forms interrelate well with other questions designed to measure the same instructor characteristic. Correlations from .77 to .94 were reported when the ratings by students in a particular class were randomly paired (Guthrie, 1954; Maslow and Zimmerman, 1956). Studies using the Illinois Course Evaluation Questionnaire, as reported by Spencer (1968) and Spencer and Aleamoni (1970), turned up high internal consistency with reliability scores averaging .93 for sixteen courses. Harvey and Barker (1970) found a correlation of .93 between student ratings on the question of the "general estimate of teacher" and the total score on the scale. Costin, Greenough and Menges (1971) obtained an .88 correlation on odd and even-numbered questionnaire items.

The Eric Clearinghouse of Higher Education Report 10 (1971), after a review of recent literature on the reliability of student ratings, concluded that, "Typical measures of split-half reliability consistently show that the instruments employed in student ratings have a high reliability. They have been checked and rechecked in different studies" (p. 12). As Miller (1974, p. 31) observes: "The evidence is clear and consistent. . . . We can count on the reliability of student rating scale. . . ."

Validity of Student Ratings

The validity of an instrument depends on whether it measures what it is supposed to measure. Applied to student ratings, the central question about their validity is whether the instructors who effectively achieve educational goals are also rated highly by students, and vice versa.

Several researchers report a moderate correlation between student ratings of instructors and their ratings by faculty colleagues. Maslow and Zimmerman (1956) and Costin (1966) found correlation coefficients of .30 to .63. Considerable agreement in the ratings by students and colleagues was also reported by Gaff (1973) and Touq and Feldhusen (1973). Another study involved eighteen instructors who taught eighteen different classes and were rated by their 488 students. Two trained classroom observers recorded interaction data. The result was considerable agreement between students and observers on the instructors' classroom performances (Touq, Feldhusen, and Halstead, 1973).

It stands to reason, and some evidence supports it, that a favorable impression by an instructor in one behavior tends favorably to infiltrate other behaviors, in the mind of the student, in the well-known "halo effect" (Hoyt, 1969). Nonetheless, Remmers (1959), giving due recognition to halo effect, believes students can and do assess the different aspects of teaching performance reliably.

Positive correlations between student examination results and student instructor ratings were reported by Cohen and Berger (1970). High correlations were also found between instructor ratings and student achievement of course objectives by Lathrop (1968). Reviewing the available correlation studies, Gage (1974) concluded that the studies "offer some support for the validity of students' ratings as indicators of how much students have learned, as objectively measured and adjusted for student aptitude" (p. 76).

This position was also taken by McKeachie (1975) at the First International Conference on Improving University Teaching. He, too, found student ratings to be valid and concluded: "There is a low but significant positive correlation between student judgments and the students' learning" (p. 75).

According to Costin, Greenough and Menges (1971), Miller (1974), and Grasha (1977), it appears that students are capable of identifying teaching practices that increase their knowledge.

CORRELATES OF STUDENT RATINGS
When faculty members discuss the subject of student ratings, a few members always argue that the ratings are sometimes influenced by factors outside the instructor's control. It is argued that the ratings are variable with class size, sex composition and class level, the instructor's professional rank, whether the course is required or elective, student grade-point average, student level of learning, and the instructor's personality.

Class Size. The belief that an instructor of a large class may tend to be the recipient of a lower rating finds support in a few studies. Lovell and Haner (1955), in a study at Grinnell College, found that instructors of classes larger than 30 students received lower ratings than instructors of smaller classes. McDaniel and Feldhusen (1970) reported the same finding. Other investigators, however, have found little or no correlation. Goodhartz (1948) found that

41

instructors at Brooklyn College of classes of less than 20 students were not rated more favorably than instructors of larger classes. No significance was reported by Solomon (1966) between class size and ratings. An interesting curvilinear relationship was found by Gage (1961) who reported that teachers with 30-39 classroom students received lower ratings than teachers with more or fewer students. Centra (1976) reported a similar finding: instructors of classes under 15 students received exceptionally high ratings, but beyond that class size the relationship between size and ratings was minimal. In classes over 100 students, a slight elevation in student ratings was noted.

Sex Composition and Class Level. Many studies have investigated the relationship between student ratings and the sex and academic year of the students. Most studies report that sex and academic year do not influence student ratings (Heilman and Armentrout, 1936; Remmers and Elliott, 1949; Lovell and Haner, 1955; Caffrey, 1969).

The Instructor's Professional Rank. There is conflicting evidence on the effect of the instructor's professional rank on student ratings. Some studies suggest that the higher the rank the higher the rating (Downie, 1952; Gage, 1961). Conversely, other studies find low-rank instructors rated highly (Goodhartz, 1948). But most studies report no relationship between the two (Guthrie, 1954; Hildebrand, Wilson and Dienst, 1971).

Required or Elective Course. Most researchers have found no significant correlation between student ratings of instructors who teach required or elective courses (Heilman and Armentrout, 1936; Goodhartz, 1948; Hildebrand, Wilson and Dienst, 1971). One study, however, produces some evidence to the contrary (Gage, 1961).

Student Grade-Point Average. Although few researchers have investigated the possible influence of this variable on student ratings, whatever studies are available conclude that grade-point average has no appreciable effect (Hildebrand, Wilson and Dienst, 1971; Kohlan, 1973).

Student Level of Learning. Much controversy has arisen in recent years over whether student ratings actually reflect the student level of learning. An important criterion of the validity of student ratings is the measure of student learning. Were there *no* positive relationship between the two, the very validity of student ratings would be called into question. However, the relationship need not be strong since so many variables, not only teaching effectiveness, affect how much a student learns.

Some researchers report no discernible relationship between ratings and learning (Heilman and Armentrout, 1936; Remmers, 1960; Voeks and French, 1960). A recent study (Rodin and Rodin,

42

1972) even found a sizeable negative correlation (-.75) between ratings and learning, which suggests that students learn least from the highly rated teachers. This study has been criticized for methodological errors, including a specially small N and the sizeable sampling error of the correlation coefficient. Further, the instructor sampling was atypical (teaching assistants in a calculus course) and the measure of student achievement (number of types of problems mastered) was unusual.

In contrast, numerous researchers have found significant positive correlations between student ratings and student learning. But the correlations are, as expected, in the low to medium range. Elliott (1950) reported a correlation of .20 and Spencer (1968) found that correlations between grades and "overall value of courses" seldom exceeded .30. Similar low correlations, from .23 to .32, were reported by Caffrey (1969). In more recent studies, two researchers at the Memorial University of Newfoundland, in Canada, obtained correlations averaging .39 in ten different courses (Sullivan and Skanes, 1973).

These positive correlations lend support to the validity of student ratings as indicators of how much students learn. Costin, Greenough and Menges (1971, p. 520) concluded from a review of almost 200 research studies that the typically low, positive correlations that occur "might better be viewed as a partial function of the better achieving students' greater interest and motivation, rather than as a mere contamination of the validity of student ratings."

The Instructor's Personality. Some academics embrace the notion that students reward the most popular instructors with the highest ratings, instructors who teach with colorful beads and flashing lights, yet whose teachir.g may lack genuine worth. This notion that the popular teacher may be the poor teacher can be self-serving. Its adherents decry the teacher who they say is more actor than teacher, an easy grader, lacks scholarship, and walks off with high student ratings. Eble (1976, p. 16) remarks wryly that "this myth even has a reverse twist: the conspicuously unpopular teacher ... must ... be good."

Many assumptions about what makes some teachers more popular than others contain large chunks of self-deception. To study the early economic theorists is assumed to be unattractive to students. It is assumed in psychology that physiology is a dead subject to students. It is assumed in English that the study of medieval literature is boring to students. The fact is, teachers in many colleges and universities are taking on these stultifying courses and making them alive to huge numbers of students. As Eble (1976, p. 17) shrewdly points out, "Gifted teachers can make subject matters attractive and interesting no matter what they are."

What empirical evidence is there about the relationship between student ratings and instructor personality? The findings are clear and consistent.

In a University of Washington study, Guthrie (1954) found that teachers who garnered the highest student ratings were also "substance" teachers, not merely entertainers. This finding is supported by Weaver (1960), Costin, Greenough and Menges (1971), Miller (1974), Seldin (1975) and McKeachie (1978).

The famed "Dr. Fox" studies (Ware and Williams, 1975) dealt mostly with how the lecturer's personality influenced student ratings. The finding that students high-rate a professor who brings theatre into the classroom was quickly seized upon by some academics as voiding entirely any value of student ratings. True, professors who show enthusiasm, humor, energy are rated more highly by students. But recognition must be given that the same professors also produce more student learning, as measured by examinations. Drama in the classroom can be an effective tool for learning.

Teaching can be viewed as a performing art. A distinctive presentation, ability to dramatize a lecture, display of enthusiasm, all tend to awaken student interest and thereby learning. Who can fault the result?

The stimulation of students by the magnetism of a professor's personality is a pedagogical approach that has been honored throughout the ages. Abelard (12th century), Da Feltra (14th century) and Comenius (16th century), each an outstanding teacher, utilized their dynamic personalities to arouse student interest.

COMMON OBJECTIONS TO STUDENT RATINGS

Several standard arguments in opposition to student ratings are voiced repeatedly at many faculty meetings.

1. *"The effectiveness of instructors cannot be judged until students have left college and gained a more worldly perspective."* This argument does not square with the evidence from three well-known studies showing that student ratings correlate well with alumni ratings. Drucker and Remmers (1951) obtained a correlation of .40 to .68, Braunstein and Benston (1953) a correlation of .85, and Centra (1974) a .75. As McKeachie (1978, p.266) remarks: "Teachers whom students think to be good are still remembered as being effective years later, and vice versa."

2. *"Student evaluations can be harsh in assessing instructors."* Actually, students are typically generous in assessing faculty performance and, if their ratings are skewed, it is on the generous side. As Hildebrand (1972, p.51) explains: "When students rate instruction on a continuum ranging through a middle value

identified on the evaluation form as 'average' performance, the mean of their ratings is higher than that 'average' value (5.5 on a 7-point scale)." This is not surprising since graphic rating scales typically result in a positive bias in ratings. But to argue against student ratings because students have a tendency to rate high also cuts the ground from under colleague rating. Colleagues tend to appraise each other even more kindly than students. A study by Centra (1977) showed that 94 percent of the instructors were rated excellent or good by their peers.

3. *"Student ratings cost too much."* The cost of student ratings depends on the extent and frequency of administration. To cut the cost, some institutions use student ratings in alternate semesters, some use a random sample of classes or students. As Eble (1970, p. 32) says pointedly: "The costs are not such that an institution could not find funds if it thought the activities involved in student evaluation were worthwhile."

4. *"An unfavorable rating of a single class can seriously diminish a professor's chance at tenure or promotion in rank."* This would constitute serious misuse of the student rating program. The cumulative effect of student evaluations over several years and including many courses is the proper index to use. Consistently favorable or unfavorable mean ratings can validly be used in personnel decisions. The American Association of University Professors, in its "Statement on Teaching Evaluation" (1974, p. 168), underscored the importance of obtaining "reliable data over a range of teaching assignments and over a period of time."

5. *"Students evaluate differently depending on their understanding of the intended use of the results."* It is argued that their ratings are more generous if students believe they will affect a professor's tenure or promotion, and less generous if they are to be used for teaching improvement. To the contrary, several studies suggest that differences in student responses are slight and inconsistent (Berkshire and Highland, 1953, and Centra, 1977).

6. *"There are better ways of evaluating teaching performance than student ratings."* Undeniably, there are other ways of evaluating teaching performance. For instance, there is classroom visitation, self-evaluation, a review of course material, use of trained evaluators, assessment of student learning. As Hildebrand (1971, p. 55) suggests, each approach has merit. But each has drawbacks, the most important being the low acceptance by faculty. Overall, Eble (1972, p. 60) believes, "Student opinion, reliably gathered and wisely used, probably has the best chance of providing useful data and of being incorporated into instructional practices." Nonetheless, it would be imprudent to limit an appraisal of classroom performance to the students. More apt to produce a fair and

reasonably accurate assessment would be to add more sources of information, for instance from peers, administrators, and from self-appraisal.

7. *"Students and faculty disagree on who is an effective teacher."* If student ratings proved to be identical with colleague ratings, the value of gathering student views would be subject to serious doubt. Similarly, if student ratings were at the opposite pole of colleague ratings, the same doubt would arise. The fact is, however, that studies show typically a positive but low correlation between student and colleague ratings. Guthrie (1954), Maslow and Zimmerman (1956), and Costin (1966) report correlations from .30 to .63, suggesting that students and colleagues apply similar criteria in the evaluation of a professor's performance. The moderate correlations suggest also that student ratings are an independent and useful contribution to teacher evaluation.

8. *"No matter how competent the students, it is simply not for them to judge their instructors."* Some academics argue that to use student ratings for tenure or promotion in rank decisions can only help to destroy the kind of instructor-student relationship necessary for effective teaching-learning. Kent (1966, p. 338) rebuts this argument by denying the prior existence of such ideal instructor-student relationship. Had it generally occurred, "the present outcry against poor teaching might not be so vociferous." The late 1960's established itself as the zenith of the student outcry in whose wake followed a swift expansion in the definition of student academic freedom. In the words of Frankel (1965, p. 246), "students have the right to bring their interests and opinions to the attention of the college." In the following years students won and exercised those rights. In the extensive literature on student evaluation, which has recently blossomed, most observers seem to have concluded that students are competent as judges of teaching and their appraisals have a place in overall teacher evaluations. Both the American Academy of Arts and Sciences and the Carnegie Commission on Higher Education have supported student ratings. At the 1975 International Conference on Improving University Teaching, in Heidelberg, Germany, Richard Miller, a leading authority in the field, told the conference that although several components were obviously preferable to one, student ratings were the "most valid, reliable and defensible goal for faculty appraisal."

Doyle (1975, p.86), summarizing research on student ratings, came to this conclusion: "Provided the data are gathered carefully, reported appropriately, and interpreted judiciously, student evaluation appears able to make a useful contribution to personnel decisions (and) course improvement...." And Seldin (1976, p. 76) urged that "the opinions of those who eat the dinner should be considered, if we want to know how it tastes."

CHOOSING AN INSTRUMENT FOR STUDENT RATINGS

Ordinarily, when an institution commences a program of student evaluation, a committee is named to devise the assessment instrument. The process is lengthy. A draft questionnaire is designed, faculty and student feedback obtained, the draft questionnaire is then redrafted and tested for reliability and validity. As Miller (1974, pp.34-35) comments: "If this exercise increases acceptablity of what is developed, then the hundreds or thousands of hours spent in developing an instrument may be justified, but normally the selection of an evaluative instrument is one of the *least* important factors in the overall evaluation process."

Instead of inventing an original student rating instrument, and in effect rediscovering the wheel, institutions have ready and immediate access to the experience and rating instruments developed at other institutions. For instance, the Purdue Rating Scale for Instruction and the Illinois Course Evaluation Questionnaire have been tested over many years and a rich inventory of normative data has been developed. The universities of Washington, Michigan (see Form 2), Cincinnati (see Form 3), Grinnell College and Illinois Benedictine College are among the leading institutions in the amassing of experience in the use of student rating forms.

The Educational Testing Service and the Center for Faculty Evaluation and Development in Higher Education, at Kansas State University, have developed rating scales and made them commercially available.

Some institutions provide a catalogue of computer-scored items for faculty members to select those most relevant to their course evaluation. There are advantages in the use of a standardized form: the possibility of computer scoring, the availability of norms for a given type of course, and some assurance that the questionnaire's content is representative and relevant and the scaling procedure and statistical analysis adequate.

Obviously, the rating scale must be congenial in nature and content to the student evaluation goals in a particular situation. And the selection of the questionnaire items will depend on local conditions as well as the course and program objectives. In general, therefore, it is sounder to adapt—not adopt—an already existing student rating scale. It is better to reshape to local conditions a preexisting assessment instrument. This is not difficult to do since most rating scales contain a surplus of items and blank spaces for the

47

insertion of locally relevant items.

As Eble (1970, p. 30) suggests, "Energies can best be spent in considering how tested materials and experience (from other institutions) can be adapted...." This view is expressed also by Miller (1974), Nadeau (1977), and McKeachie (1978).

The adaptive process can begin with a working definition of

Form 1.
STUDENT DESCRIPTION OF TEACHERS, SHORT FORM

INSTRUCTOR _____

DEPARTMENT _____

COURSE NUMBER OR TITLE _____

I. The following items reflect some of the ways teachers can be described in and out of the classroom. For the instructor named above, please circle the number which indicates the degree to which you feel each item is descriptive of him or her. In some cases, the statement may not apply to this individual. In these cases, check *Does not apply or don't know* for that item.

	Not at all Descriptive	*Very Descriptive*	*Doesn't apply or don't know*
1. Has command of the subject, presents material in an analytic way, contrasts various points of view, discusses current developments, and relates topics to other areas of knowledge.	1 2 3	4 5 6 7	( )

2. Makes himself clear, states objectives, summarizes major points, presents material in an organized manner, and provides emphasis.
3. Is sensitive to the response of the class, encourages student participation, and welcomes questions and discussion.
4. Is available to and friendly towards students, is interested in students as individuals, is himself respected as a person, and is valued for advice not directly related to the course.
5. Enjoys teaching, is enthusiastic about his subject, makes the course exciting, and has self-confidence.

(Additional items may be presented by instructor and/or department)

II.
1. How does the instructor of this course compare with other teachers you have had at *this school?*

Among the very worst		*About average*			*Among the very best*	
1	2	3	4	5	6	7

2. How does the instructor of this course compare with other teachers you have had in *this department?*

Among the very worst		*About average*			*Among the very best*	
1	2	3	4	5	6	7

You are invited to comment further on the course and/or effectiveness of this instructor especially in areas not covered by the questions.

Source: Developed by Robert C. Wilson and Evelyn R. Dienst, Center for Research and Development in Higher Education, University of California, Berkeley. Form SSF-3. Reproduced by permission of the authors.

teaching effectiveness as related to the goals of the institutions. The help of some faculty members in the psychology and education departments can be enlisted in designing and testing the questionnaire, as insurance that the adapted instrument actually measures what it is supposed to measure and is reliable. Of particular importance, is the encouragement of open discussion on the subjects of teaching performance and student evaluations, in which administration, faculty and students freely partake, so that joint confidence can be built for the rating program finally adopted. At all stages of program development, decisions must be openly arrived at as well as the reasoning behind them.

In the words of TDR Associates (1975, pp. 30–31): "If students, faculty and administrators...have actively contributed to the planning of each step, they will 'own' the program that emerges. Only this perceived ownership can lend real acceptance in the implementation stages."

The integrity of the final program depends absolutely on its honest assembly. Lacking this, students will lack motivation to give the questionnaire their considered attention, faculty members will resent the student ratings as unfair or devoid of significance, and administrators will be unable to consider the ratings properly in personnel decisions.

STUDENT PERCEPTIONS OF LEARNING AND TEACHING

The items on this questionnaire ask you to comment on various aspects of your course.

The questionnaire has eight brief parts. The first part is intended to assess your perception of your own learning; the second part is your perception of characteristics related to instructor effectiveness. Other parts are not evaluative but are intended to assess aspects of teacher style; for example, either a high or low degree of structure may be effective.

Thank you for taking the time to fill this form out thoughtfully. Your answers and comments will help your teacher improve the course.

Date: _____   Your Class Standing (Circle):

Course: _____   Fr   Soph   Jr   Sr   Grad

Instructor_____

If not applicable, leave blank
1 = almost never or almost nothing   4 = often or much
2 = seldom or little   5 = very often
3 = occasionally or moderate   6 = almost always or a great deal

IMPACT ON STUDENTS

1. My intellectual curiosity has been stimulated by this course.
   Comments:

2. I am learning how to think more clearly about the area of this course.
   Comments:

3. I am learning how to read materials in this area more effectively.
   Comments:

4. I am acquiring a good deal of knowledge about the subject.
   Comments:

5. The course is making a significant contribution to my self-understanding.
   Comments:

6. The course is increasing my interest in learning more about this area.

INSTRUCTOR EFFECTIVENESS

7. The instructor is enthusiastic.
   Comments:

8. The instructor gives good examples of the concepts.
   Comments:

9. The instructor goes into too much detail.
   Comments:

10. The instructor is helpful when students are confused.
    Comments:

11. The instructor seems knowledgeable in many areas.
    Comments:

RAPPORT

12. The instructor knows students' names.
    Comments:

13. The instructor is friendly.
    Comments:

GROUP INTERACTION

14. Students volunteer their own opinions.
    Comments:

15. Students discuss one another's ideas.
    Comments:

16. Students feel free to disagree with the instructor.
    Comments:

DIFFICULTY

17. The instructor makes difficult assignments.
    Comments:

18. The instructor asks for a great deal of work.
    Comments:

STRUCTURE

19. The instructor plans class activities in detail.
    Comments:

20. The instructor follows an outline closely.
    Comments:

FEEDBACK

21. The instructor keeps students informed of their progress.
    Comments:

22. The instructor tells students when they have done a particularly good job.
    Comments:

23. Tests and papers are graded and returned promptly.
    Comments:

NOTICE!!! THIS SCALE IS DIFFERENT!!!

STUDENT RESPONSIBILITY

If not applicable, leave blank   3 = in-between
1 = definitely false   4 = more true than false
2 = more false than true   5 = definitely true

24. I had a strong desire to take this course.
    Comments:

25. I actively participate in class discussions.
    Comments:

26. I consciously try to make a tie-in between what I am learning through the course
    and my own experience.
    Comments:

27. I attend class regularly.
    Comments:

28. I utilize all the learning opportunities provided in the course.
Comments:

29. I have created learning experiences for myself in connection with the course.
Comments:

30. I have helped classmates learn.
Comments:

OVERALL EVALUATION

Indicate your evaluation of characteristics below, using numbers based on the following scale:

1. Poor   2. Fair   3. Good   4. Very Good   5. Excellent

31. Rate the instructor's general teaching effectiveness for you.
Comments:

32. Rate the value of the course as a whole to you.
Comments:

Source: Developed by W. J. McKeachie,
University of Michigan.
Reproduced by permission.

Form 3.
A SAMPLE QUESTIONNAIRE FOR THE CLASSROOM

For the following questions, you are to rate how you feel about each method as used in all of your classes and how the instructor in this class used the method. If a method is non-applicable to another class, indicate by placing NA after the question.

Other classes   This class

1. I would rate the lectures as:
   a. Extremely interesting
   b. Interesting
   c. Of average interest
   d. Below average in interest
   e. Boring

2. I would rate the in-class discussions as:
   a. Extremely interesting
   b. Interesting
   c. Of average interest
   d. Below average interest
   e. Boring

3. I would rate the text book as:
   a. Difficult
   b. Above average in difficulty
   c. Of average difficulty
   d. Below average in difficulty
   e. Easy

4. I would rate the outside reading as:
   a. Difficult
   b. Above average in difficulty
   c. Of average difficulty
   d. Below average difficulty
   e. Easy

5. The exams were:
   a. Hard
   b. Of average difficulty
   c. Easy
   d. Other (Please indicate)

6. If any method was given a rating of "average interest", "average difficulty", or less, indicate at least one reason why the method was given such a rating.

7. What is the one thing that you would do to improve each of the methods used?
   a. Lectures
   b. In-class discussions
   c. Textbooks
   d. Study guides
   e. Outside readings
   f. Exams

8. In the space provided, indicate whether these methods were generally adequate for allowing you to learn content. If no, why do you feel they were inadequate?

	Adequate	Inadequate
Lectures		
In-class discussions		
Textbook		
Study guides		
Outside readings		
Exams		

9. What additional methods might have been used to help you learn better?

54

10. For the lectures, outside readings and the textbook indicate what topic you enjoyed the most and the topic you enjoyed the least.
    Lectures
    Outside readings
    Textbook

11. ·Besides content, what would be three other skills a course like this should teach?

12. What 5 topics do you feel the text covered well? Not well?

13. What outside readings would you *not* recommend be used in the course again?

14. Three traits I *liked most* in the instructor were:

15. Three traits I *liked least* in the instructor were:

16. I would recommend this course to my friends.
    a. Yes
    b. No
    c. Please specify the reason for your answer.

17. List three things you *liked* about the course.

18. List three things you *disliked* about the course.

19. Based on your analysis of your learning needs and desires, what would have been the ideal way to have run the course during the quarter?

For each of the items on this sheet, rate your instructor using the seven point rating scale listed below. You are to rate your instructor in two ways. *In the column marked "expectations" rate your instructor on each item in terms of how well you expect a teacher to behave on each item* based on your preferences for such behaviors. Place the number *corresponding to each rating category in the space provided.* After rating your expectations for each item, rate the observed behavior of your teacher in terms of how the teacher compares to the average ability of all the other instructors you have had. *Try to be as honest and objective in your ratings as possible.*

Excellent	Very Good	Good	Satisfactory	Fair	Poor	Very Poor
7	6	5	4	3	2	1

Expectations Observed

20. Discusses points of view other than his own.
21. Contrasts implications of various theories.
22. Explains clearly.
23. Is well-prepared.
24. Encourages class discussion.
25. Invites students to share their knowledge and experiences.
26. Has a genuine interest in students.
27. Is friendly toward students.
28. Is a dynamic and energetic person.
29. Has an interesting style of presentation.

55

30. Encourages students to pursue further study in the field.
31. Demonstrates knowledge of subject matter.

32. If any Item was given a rating of *"satisfactory" or less, give at least one reason* why you gave that rating.

Please rate the extent to which you did the following things (questions 33-36) in this class compared to other classes you have taken. Use the seven point rating scale listed above.

33. Participating in class discussion on issues the instructor raised.
34. Preparing for class.
35. Asking questions.
36. Sharing my knowledge and experiences with other students and the teacher.
37. Besides the above, what are one-two things you could have done to make this a better class?

Source: Developed by Anthony F. Grasha,
University of Cincinnati.
Reproduced by permission.

Form of the Questionnaire

The three key decisions regarding the form of the questionnaire are: 1) flexibility, 2) length/format, 3) selection of included items.

1. *Flexibility.* There is probably no single questionnaire suitable to every department or institution. Different instruments are needed to evaluate different courses and produce different information. With this in mind, there is nonetheless a distinct advantage in utilizing a common instrument assessing a range of teaching styles and subject areas: the advantage of providing meaningful comparative data.

At the University of Washington, for instance, the faculty members select one of five versions of a questionnaire as most suitable for their course. Each version serves the same end by seeking information which 1) can be considered by administrators in personnel decisions, 2) can be used by the faculty member to improve teaching performance, and 3) can inform students about courses and instructors. By offering five versions, flexibility is built into the program, yet by containing many comparable items, reliability is assured.

Similarly, Purdue University's "Cafeteria System" integrates three separate activities, instructional evaluation, assistance, and reward, into a single program of instructional improvement. One virtue of the "Cafeteria System" is its capacity to accommodate differences in instructional strategies. Each instructor selects a number of rating scale items from a "catalogue" of 200 or more items. The selected items are then added to the "core" items in the assessment of faculty and from the computer emerges a tailor-made rating instrument. Standards and norms are available so that faculty members can compare ratings on items they selected with other faculty members who selected the same items. And the core items provide rating comparisons for all the participating faculty members.

2. *Length/Format.* How many items in the questionnaire? If too short, it may not produce enough information, if too long, it may produce student resentment, to say nothing of the added logistical problem of tabulation. Some standard instruments are available in short, medium and long form.

For personnel decisions, a short form containing from five to ten items, will ordinarily suffice. For faculty members interested in improving classroom performance, a medium (15–20 items) or long form (30–35 items) will serve their purpose. Between ten and twenty minutes should be the maximum time needed by students to complete the questionnaire.

It is preferable that the form not exceed two pages, have a clean, attractive appearance, also appear important enough to command a thoughtful student response. Instructions must be simple and direct and the response area adequate.

3. *Selection of Included Items.* Many rating forms ask questions about instructional practices, including, for instance, student views on whether the teacher is well-prepared for class, has an interesting style of presentation, or explains clearly. Grasha (1977) urges the importance of giving students a reference point so that they can compare instructor performance. Such reference can be, for instance, the best, worst, or average teacher, or even other teachers in the department.

A major development in student ratings is to place in the core of compulsory items questions about the general characteristics of the teacher or the course. Typical questions might be: "How do you rate this teacher in comparison to others you have had in the department? In comparison to all others you have had in the institution as a whole?"

Several studies (Sullivan and Skanes, 1974; Centra, 1976) suggest that these global ratings tend to be more closely related to student learning than questions on specific instructional behavior. Global ratings have the advantage by not being limited to any instructional style.

If student ratings are to be used to improve classroom performance, it is advisable to include several open-end questions so that students can respond to the questions in their own words. Examples: "List the three traits you liked most about the instructor."

"If you were teaching this course, what is the first thing you would change?"

PLANNING PROGRAMS OF INSTRUCTOR EVALUATION

To develop a successful evaluation program requires several key decisions. Any program which neglects to spell out these decisions will almost certainly falter in its execution.

Guidelines and Strategy

Following, are some general guidelines and strategy suggestions to help implement a successful student evaluation program.

Miller (1972) suggests a six-step approach: (1) Obtain administrative support for the evaluation plan. (2) Allow sufficient time to implement the system, work hard, develop a solid research base and show enthusiasm for the evaluation program. (3) Conduct dry runs to improve the rating instrument and reduce the anxiety level among faculty. (4) Anticipate faculty resistance and deal with it positively, and focus energy on the use of student ratings for teaching improvement as well as personnel decisions. (5) Hold open faculty forums during the developmental stage of the rating instrument and the student newspaper and other student groups should be encouraged to attend. (6) Provide sufficient time for the overall process of implementation—a term or two years is reasonable—and spell out follow-up procedures to evaluate the system itself. In conclusion, Miller advises (p. 20): "Strategies for implementation need time, careful planning, openness, administrative support, and probably a bit of luck. The content needs to be good and adequate research should be evident on what is proposed."

Eble (1970) offers a ten-step approach: (1) Obtain faculty cooperation. (2) Determine purposes, objectives and uses for evaluation data. (3) Determine evaluation methods and procedures. (4) Decide who, what, where, and when the evaluation system will be implemented, as well as the student role in the total assessment system. (5) Establish a fixed office to administer the evaluation program. (6) Keep all segments of the campus community informed on a continuous basis. (7) Determine the financing of the evaluation system. (8) Maintain student and faculty interest. (9) Conduct follow-up studies to assess the effectiveness of the program and improve it. (10) Tie evaluation to other efforts for the recognition, reward and improvement of instruction.

The approaches suggested by Miller and Eble contain large areas of common advice. Their experience, and their study of others' experience, urge the wisdom of proceeding slowly, carefully, openly, and laying the groundwork for each step in the program.

The following outline was developed by Hildebrand, Wilson, and

Dienst (1971, pp. 46–48) at the University of California, Berkeley. It is a checklist of tasks to be undertaken and options to be considered by program planners in the implementation of their evaluation programs.

Figure 2.
Tasks and Options in Evaluating Faculty

PURPOSES
Feedback to instructor for self-improvement
Data for making salary, promotion, and tenure decisions
Information to assist students in choosing courses and instructors
A combination of the above

SCOPE
Number of teachers
Small number (e.g., all of one department)
Medium number (e.g., all eligible for tenure)
Large number (e.g., all in the institution)
Number of classes
One per instructor per advancement period
One per instructor per year
Each once per advancement period
Each every other year, or every year
Number of students
Random sample of X students (large classes only?)
X percent of class (large classes only?)
All (but with minimum of X returns to qualify for interpretation?)
Kinds of courses
Undergraduate credit courses
All except seminars and field research courses
All (including noncredit and extension?)

FORMS
Style
Structured check-off items
Open-ended essay items
Coverage
Teaching only
Teaching and course
Teaching, course, and student data (demographic, objectives, values)
Format
Optical scanning sheets
Mark sense sheets
Porto-punch cards
Duplicated questionnaire with key punch
Duplicated questionnaire with hand tally
Length
Short (1-25 items)
Medium (26-50 items)
Long (>50 items)

Sources
    External (for example, another campus, Center for Research and
        Development in Higher Education, Berkeley)
    Local committee (faculty, administrative, student, combination)
    Instructor
    A combination of the above

ADMINISTRATION AND DATA GATHERING
Time of distribution
    Early in course
    Late in course
    With final examination
    After course
Method of distribution
    Instructor
    Student representative
    Administrative representative
    With registration packets
    Mail
Method of return
    Collected by instructor
    Collected by student representative
    Collected by administrative representative
    Mailed to a central office

DATA REDUCTION
Persons involved
    Instructor
    Department
    Committee (student, faculty, administrative, combination)
    Central office
Method
    Summarization by computer, with norms and variances
    Hand-tabulation and individual case study
    Summarization of open-ended data

INTERPRETATION OF DATA
Persons involved
    Instructor
    Department
    Committee (student, faculty, administrative, combination)
    Central office
Basis
    Individual case study
    Departmental norms
    College or school norms
    Campus norms

PROVISION FOR CHALLENGE
    None
    By instructor
    By students or department
    Procedures

DISSEMINATION AND REPORTING
    To instructor only
    To instructor and departmental chairman or committee
    To instructor, department, and administration
    To university community at a central location
    To university community by sale or general distribution

Source: Center for Research and Development in Higher Education,
          University of California, Berkeley (1971).
          Developed by M. Hildebrand, R. Wilson, and E. Dienst.

ADMINISTERING THE RATING FORMS

Unfortunately, too many student rating programs are thwarted by defective administrative machinery. Among the common defects is a sporadic rating schedule, a biasing effect by improper instructions, a lack of standards which voids the possibility of meaningful interpretation. These and other defects need eradication so that standardized and defensible procedures can increase the validity and the usefulness of the gathered information.

A suggested first step in administering student ratings is a "dry run" on a representative sample of students. This gives both students and instructor needed experience. It can also provoke analytical discussion about the content, structure and administration of the appraisal instrument itself. This can lead to corrective modifications of the rating forms and administrative procedure.

How and when should the questionnaire be administered? One procedure in use at many colleges and universities has proved simple and effective. Students fill out the rating forms two weeks before the term ends, and before final examinations. The forms are distributed and completed within a single week. A statement of instructions is read to the students by a class assistant. During the reading of the instructions and the completion of the forms by the students, the instructor remains outside the classroom. At the end of a fixed period, ordinarily no more than 15 minutes, the assistant collects the forms, places them in an envelope which is labeled with course title and number, and in view of the students seals the envelope. The envelope is then secured in the dean's office or other controlled place. Although the forms are processed within two weeks, the results are not publicized until after the issuance of final grades.

It is crucial to maintain distance between the instructor and the students who are evaluating him. The students must feel secure in their anonymity. As Eble (1970, p. 24) cautions: "Filling out the questionnaire under the eyes of the faculty member...may inhibit or distort the response." Not surprisingly, a study at the University of Kentucky confirmed this caution. Kirchner (1969) reported significantly higher student ratings when the instructor was in the classroom than when he was absent.

Should a single rating form be used throughout the institution? The obvious advantage is that it produces an overall teaching estimation, and it permits comparisons of instructors and of departments. However, the disadvantages can be manifold. For instance, the purposes of the evaluation may differ from one department to another, or within a department. Also, exceptionally small classes or laboratory courses are ill-suited to survey techniques. Since policies and practices, to say nothing of campus politics, vary from institution to institution, the decision on whether a single or multiple rating form should be used should be made locally.

Is there any scheduling of ratings that gives optimum results? The question can be approached this way: for a rating program to remain effective students must give carefully considered responses. The danger is real that response quality and quantity will suffer a decline if students in every class, every semester, are asked to complete rating forms. In fact, if the number of completed questionnaires in any class falls below 70–75 percent, the results may be questionable.

"Evaluation fatigue," which expresses in a pithy phrase the direct effect of over-evaluation, is not uncommon at some colleges and universities. The ailment disappears when evaluation of every course, every semester, is replaced by evaluation every year or two.

INTERPRETING THE RATING FORMS

A chronic and frustrating problem accompanying student ratings lies in their interpretation. Frequently, instructors have no idea whether their ratings are good, average or poor, or how their ratings compare with other instructors' ratings.

Some colleges and universities have solved this problem by issuing to each instructor an interpretation manual, which contains the norms (average scores, percentiles, etc.) and makes possible performance comparisons. If the normative comparison is compatible with the specific characteristics of a given teacher and course (for example, large, introductory lecture courses), an instructor will be able to make much more sense of his student ratings.

If the student ratings are going to be used by the administration for personnel decisions, then global or overall ratings should be used. And the decisions should be based on ratings in several courses over several years, never on a single course rating.

If the purpose of the student ratings is to improve teaching performance, then they should be interpreted for specific teaching behaviors. Some institutions help the instructor who wants to improve his classroom performance. At Kansas State University, for instance, a trained individual helps instructors in the interpretation of their ratings, helps clarify and resolve problems, and assures that proper corrective action is taken. A study by Aleamoni (1974) found that student ratings improved teaching performance when the ratings were analyzed and discussed with a trained evaluation person. McKeachie (1975) also reported improved teaching after the student ratings were interpreted by a person with rating expertise. It is an understandable shock to a high-rated instructor when he discovers that a few students low-rated him. But the experienced instructor knows that students react to him individually and some individuals, for one reason or another, are turned off by something he does or says.

Who Should Receive Feedback?

That depends on the purpose of the evaluation program. Also a few other considerations enter. Students, for instance, who have given of themselves in time and carefully thought out responses to the questionnaire, are clearly entitled to learn something of the results, if for no other reason than to hold their interest and loyalty to the evaluation program. Against the student interest must be balanced the instructor's right to privacy and confidentiality. The fact is, there is considerable faculty opposition to student ratings as a violation of academic freedom and an unwarranted intrusion into classroom privacy. This has appreciatively slowed the adoption of evaluation programs. It has also brought about some institutional attempts at balancing the equities. At Kansas State University, for instance, *before* the evaluation program is administered, the instructor signs a release which identifies who will be entitled to view the results. At William Rainey Harper College, in Illinois, the student scale has 23 items for diagnostic purposes and one overall item for personnel decisions, and only the instructor has access to all the findings. More colleges and universities today provide the opportunity to faculty members to review and comment on their evaluations. The comments are attached to the ratings so that faculty committees and administrators using the ratings for personnel decisions also have the benefit of the comments.

Each method is a facing up to the issue of academic freedom while guarding the usefulness of the student ratings. Regardless of method, however, the introduction of some faculty control over who views the results can only reduce faculty opposition to the student evaluation program.

Summary and Conclusions

The opinion can safely be hazarded that student evaluations will never be a panacea for the ailments of higher education, but they can heighten teacher effectiveness and thereby improve the quality of undergraduate education. There is enough empirical evidence to indicate that student ratings provide reliable and valid information. Many studies find that student ratings really zero in on the quality of instruction, and are not distracted by the teacher's entertainment virtues or grades received.

If one thing is clear, it is that the primary goal of student ratings should be the improvement of classroom performance. And the likelihood of improvement increases when the instructor can turn to the expertise of another person to interpret the student ratings and discuss the specific areas open to improvement.

Student ratings have the additional raison d'etre of administrative promotion and tenure decisions. In this area, however, the ratings are a necessary but hardly sufficient basis for such decisions. Colleague and administrator appraisal, as well as self-appraisal, are other useful sources of information.

Institutions conducting an initial exploration of student evaluation should rely on the experience and rating forms already developed by such universities as Purdue, Princeton, Washington, Northwestern, and California at Berkeley. Such rating forms can be adapted to fit local needs. Adaption is relatively easy and if accompanied at each stage by open discussion on the campus can pay an extra dividend in heightened confidence in the benefits of the rating program.

In adapting someone else's rating form, three decisions are crucial: (1) How to make the rating instrument flexible to serve several purposes. (2) How many items are needed and what form should they take. (3) Which questions need answering.

Lapses in these decisions can prove fatal to the program, or at best will flaw it. The checklist developed by Hildebrand, Wilson, and Dienst (1971) can be helpful.

Standardizing the administrative procedures dealing with student ratings is essential. Conducting a "dry run" on a representative sample of students is recommended. Student ratings will be more accurate if completed without the intimidating presence of the instructor in the classroom. Student confidence in the program will thereby also be increased.

The ratings themselves will be more accurately interpreted if the instructors are given normative data. If the ratings are intended for personnel decisions, global ratings are needed and a minimum of 70 percent of the students in the class should complete the questionnaire. If the ratings are intended to improve instruction, they should be interpreted for specific teaching behaviors. And improved instruction is more likely when the results are analyzed and discussed by an evaluative expert.

The conclusion of the Costin, Greenough, and Menges study (1971, p. 531) reads as follows: "We wish to emphasize that student ratings of undergraduate teaching fall far short of a complete assessment of an instructor's teaching contribution. . . . Nevertheless, if teaching performance is to be evaluated, either for purposes of pay and promotion, or for individual improvement, a systematic measure of student attitudes, opinions and observations can hardly be ignored. The data which have been reviewed strongly suggest that the use of formal student ratings provides a reasonable way of measuring student reaction."

The writer adds "amen."

Chapter 4

Colleague Evaluation

In appraising a faculty member's performance, two roles can be played by his colleagues. First, they can serve as reviewers of the bits and pieces of evidence and campus scuttlebut, carefully distinguishing between the two. From this review, they can form a collective judgment about the level of the faculty member's competence, and share their judgment with other decision-makers and the faculty member under review. Second, as a result of their own observation of their colleague's classroom performance, they can provide judgmental information to other review groups.

THE COLLECTIVE JUDGMENT ROLE

Typically, this role turns up on campuses using departmental or institutional personnel committees as reviewers of evidence. Beaird (1975, pp. 43–44) has suggested some important but, unfortunately, frequently overlooked guidelines:

"1. The charge to the committee must be explicit. This charge should include a statement of their responsibilities, necessary preparation, reporting instructions, and the timeline within which they must function.

2. The committee should initially review the charge and seek any clarification needed.

3. If not specifically provided, the committee must establish and make clear the rules of evidence under which it will operate. These rules should attend to criteria, their differential importance, and procedures to follow if additional evidence is required.

4. The committee must establish a decision-making process and periodically check to see that it is being followed.

5. Finally, avenues of appeal and/or rebuttal should be clarified."

THE ROLE OF PROVIDING EVIDENCE

There are two avenues that are windows on a faculty member's performance: examination of instructional material and classroom visitation.

Examination of Instructional Material

It seems self-evident that a review of instructional and other related material can be useful in judging teaching performance. Regrettably, few colleges and universities go in for such review since its mere suggestion has caused faculty eruptions about academic freedom and violations of classroom privacy. Nonetheless, an examination of instructional material would include judgments on:

1) *Course syllabus.* Is it current, relevant to the course outline? Have creative teaching aids been developed? Is the course syllabus at an appropriate difficulty level?

2) *Homework assignments.* Are they effectively coordinated with the syllabus? Will they produce a challenging and meaningful experience for the students? Are they appropriate in frequency, length?

3) *Course objectives.* Do they represent an appropriate mastery of the subject? Has the instructor communicated the objectives to the students? Do the objectives dovetail with the department's overall objectives? Will course completion logically prepare students for more complex courses in the subject?

4) *Examinations.* Are the examinations consistent with the course objectives? Do they reflect the important aspects of the subject? Are the tests promptly returned and the subject matter of wrong answers again explained? Do the grades follow an acceptable distribution pattern? Are the students knowledgeable of the bases for the final grades?

5) *Learning approaches.* Are the learning approaches (texts, reading lists, films, demonstrations, assignments, lectures) suitable to the course objectives? Which are used, which are not? What are the instructor's techniques in motivating his students? Are they appropriate? Are they effectively organized for the subject and the desired learning level?

6) *Textbooks and handouts.* Are they appropriate to the course level? Do they support the course objectives? Are they in general agreement with the department's standards?

7) *Reading and reading lists.* Do they supplement the lecture notes and class discussion? Are they relevant and current? Are they challenging to the students? Do they reflect contemporary views and the weight of evidence in the subject?

8) *Course content.* Is it consistent with the contemporary

knowledge of the subject? Is the instructor's treatment fair and lively? Does he offer a full and accurate presentation of conflicting views and evidence?

9) *Lecture notes.* Do they faithfully follow the course outline? Are they logically organized and sequential? Do they supplement the text and other class material? Do they support the course objectives? Do they reflect current subject knowledge?

10) *Overview.* From the above scrutiny what would be your overall judgment on the adequacy of the course preparation and the concern of the instructor for his classroom work? What would be your judgment as to how he rates in these areas with other instructors in the department, and in the institution as a whole?

No question, faculty colleagues and department chairmen are in a good position to assess instructional material. But extreme care must be exercised to reach a reasonably accurate interpretation if it is to be applied to personnel decisions or teaching improvement. The objectives of fairness and nailed-down precision should be carefully and persistently wooed and the final judgments on the instructional material should supplement other data in the evaluation process.

Miller (1975, p. 26) suggests that one successful approach to the evaluation of instructional material is to "have a colleague teaching the same subject and another teacher outside the teacher's discipline go over course outlines and other distributed materials and make judgments about their accuracy, academic soundness, relationship with the course objectives, and their level. Results of the study should be shared with the teacher and copies should go to the dean and department head."

A handful of institutions have developed forms containing criteria for this slice of peer evaluation. The criteria include the usefulness of materials, extent of innovation, appropriateness of syllabus, fairness of examinations, and distribution of grades. The answers are solicited in general terms. (See Miller, 1975, p. 34, for example.)

Classroom Visitation

There is ample literature on colleague evaluation by classroom visitation. Morton (1961, p. 122) commends this method as "effectively used ... when (it) involves friendliness and interest as well as a critical and instructional purpose." He urges that the observer be supplied in advance with course outline or the material-of-the-day and the procedures intended for classroom use.

Bayley (1967, pp. 116–117) concurs in the merit of colleague evaluation. He lists the following benefits: "First, colleagues will provide as trustworthy critics of classroom activity and course organization as can be found. They will provide teachers with the essential element of feedback. . . . Second, colleague observation will provide the best information possible for the rewarding of the superior teaching and the discipline of inadequate teaching."

Classroom observation is enthusiastically supported by Megaw (1967), who suggests naming a special committee-of-instruction, to consist of elected faculty members, each making classroom visits and reporting on teaching effectiveness. Megaw urges colleges and universities to support the committee-of-instruction by allocating up to three percent of total faculty expenses for the committee's work.

Colleague evaluation is similarly endorsed by Hodgkinson (1971), on the ground that it provides substantial data for clinical and statistical interpretation. This, in turn, encourages improved teaching and helps to establish criteria for assessment.

Other supporters of classroom visitation by colleagues include Estrin and Goodwin (1962), Smart (1965), Gaff and Wilson (1971), Eble (1972) and Miller (1974).

Opponents of classroom visitation are also numerous. Gage (1961, p. 19) argues that "when the teacher knows he is being watched by someone whose opinion will determine his promotion or salary, his performance may depend more on his nerve than on his teaching skill."

Winthrop's (1966) opposition stems from his concern that teachers, who are out of step with the politics, dress or values of colleagues, no matter how effective as teachers, will tend to be unfavorably judged in a classroom visit. This will tend to ossify teachers into intellectual conformity.

Hunter (1969) in a position paper denounced classroom visitation as a threat to faculty morale. Whatever merit there is in classroom visitation, in Hunter's view, is heavily outweighed by the inevitable suspicion, distrust and schism between teacher and observer.

Although many educators have fired off position papers supporting or opposing classroom observation, few have actually conducted studies of the reliability and validity of colleague visitation. Some of the studies are worth noting.

Hildebrand, Wilson and Dienst (1971) found close agreement between faculty and student ratings of the best and worst teachers at the University of California, Berkeley. A review of the literature convinced Dwyer (1972) that students and faculty are bedfellows in their general agreement on teacher ratings; but ratings by department administrators tended to be more generous as their years of acquaintanceship with the teacher lengthened. And the administrator ratings correlated less highly with student ratings.

Gromisch (1972) compared the ratings by students and depart-

69

ment chairmen of 24 university teachers and found low correlation for overall assessment as well as 38 specifics for each teacher.

In a review of the findings by numerous researchers, Kulik (1974) concluded that colleague ratings were in general agreement with student ratings of a teacher.

Centra (1975) studied colleague ratings based on classroom observation as compared to student ratings. Each instructor was observed and rated twice by three colleagues for a total of six separate ratings. Both specific instructional practices (e.g. instructor's effective use of class time) and global items (e.g. instructor's overall effectiveness) were included in the study. Centra found colleague ratings exceptionally generous: 94 percent of the instructors were rated excellent or good. Student ratings for the same instructors were also generous but not as lavish. On a 5-point scale, the average colleague rating was 4.47, the average student rating 3.98. Centra believes the colleague ratings less reliable than the student ratings due to a built-in colleague bias and an insufficient number of participating colleagues.

In a widely publicized position paper, the American Association of University Professors offers at best only cautious and provisional support for classroom visitation as part of the teacher evaluative process. In a summary of its viewpoint, the AAUP (1974, p. 168) stated: "Careful observation over a period of time . . . may be useful in evaluating instruction and in fostering effective teaching."

Actually, a solitary observation of a teacher's classroom performance may not represent the teacher's customary performance. Periodic observation by one or more colleagues will more likely produce representative teaching performance.

With this in mind, Centra (1977, p. 99) believes that ratings based *primarily* on classroom observation are generally "not . . . reliable enough to use in making decisions on tenure and promotion—at least not until faculty members invested much more time in visitations. . . ."

Reliability increases, however, when several colleagues independently visit a classroom several times. Their collective judgments may be depended on for more accuracy than any single judgment. Any individual bias tends to be diluted. Additionally, reliability can be increased by training colleagues to be more effective observers, to know the criteria of effective teaching.

There are problems, admittedly, in using colleague visitation as a basis for making personnel decisions.

First, at most colleges and universities the necessary mutual trust, respect and support are lacking, in part or in whole, to permit decent colleague evaluation.

70

Second, classroom visitation is often beset by problems of sampling and rater unreliability.

Third, colleague bias on what constitutes good teaching often clouds his observance of teaching performance. In this respect, Ryans (1967) identifies three diverse patterns of teaching behavior: (a) friendly, understanding, sympathetic; (b) responsible, business-like, systematic; (c) stimulating, imaginative. All three patterns are widely and effectively used, but a classroom observer may incline toward one and discount the others.

Fourth, the instructor's performance may be weakened by anxiety or influenced by an unusual amount of preparation.

Fifth, the investment in time, energy and money required to develop and implement the colleague visitation method is unattractive to institution administrations.

Sixth, the sticky problems inherent in any observational system manifest themselves in classroom visitation: (a) what shall be observed, (b) can observers agree on what they have seen, (c) are the observers trained and qualified for the test, (d) do the benefits outweigh the costs.

Seventh, classroom visitation flies in the face of academic tradition and the faculty resistance is proverbial. Eble (1972, p. 61) finds the resistance rooted in "suspicions towards the visitor's intentions, uneasiness caused by a stranger in the classroom, violation of dignity or professional standing and doubts about the outcome of the observation. . . ."

Eighth, it is natural for a colleague to be discomfited by the need to be critical of a fellow teacher who is also his friend. Academia is no stranger to backscratching. In such important matters as tenure, promotion, salary increase, why flagellate when you can stroke and everybody comes away happy?

Ninth, in the name of fairness some institutions have adopted excessive methods. At one college, for instance, the team visiting the classroom consisted of academic dean, department chairman and two department members. Not once but five times during the semester the team came to observe. Miller (1974, p. 20) disposes of such methods as "overkill in terms of professional time . . . and structure."

Generally, institutions have achieved greater success with visitation teams when the purpose is to improve teaching performance rather than personnel decision. Then, the reliability of a colleague's rating diminishes as an issue and the teacher's opposition to the visit is deflated.

Experience suggests the wisdom of joining younger and older faculty as a working team to evaluate each other's classroom performance. Another successful method is the creation of a team of three or four faculty members, which meets with the teacher to discuss goals, problems, personal objectives, then observes several times in the classroom, and finally meets with the teacher or his class to discuss findings and recommendations.

Even encouraging a free exchange of ideas among the faculty may help to improve instruction. In some departments, monthly meetings are held in which the faculty can discuss methods of dealing with special teaching/learning problems. In other departments, one teacher receives the designation of master teacher and a lighter teaching load so that he can serve as classroom observer to his colleagues, and offer criticism and recommendations for their improvement. The master teacher is chosen for his reputation, his students' performance on standardized tests, or teaching experience, and the designation can be rotated annually in the department.

Colleague evaluation is more likely to strengthen instruction if (1) the instructor does not get defensive about his teaching, (2) the visiting colleague offers his views in a detached, objective, informal, factual, descriptive manner, (3) the visiting colleague enjoys the benefits of interpersonal training before the classroom visit, (4) the institution's administration openly nourishes candor and support in faculty relationships.

Simply opening the classroom to visitation by colleagues, administrators or outside experts is no guarantee of solid judgments of teaching performance by the visitors. Careful planning prior to the visit is essential.

What, specifically, are the traits, the characteristics to look for in teaching performance? What questions will help zero in on the quintessential teacher?

1. *Instructor knowledge.* Does the instructor exhibit content mastery, breadth, depth? Has he religiously kept abreast of the discipline? Is his subject expertise appropriately demonstrated in the classroom? Is his material appropriate to the level of the course? And appropriate to the level of student preparation?

2. *Method of instruction.* Does the classroom presentation exhibit clear signs of planning and organization? Is the material clearly presented? Is class time used efficiently? Does the instructor adapt methods to meet new situations? Is special or supplementary material (e.g. handouts) effectively handled by the instructor? How much critical thinking and analysis by students in the class does he elicit?

3. *Instructor-student rapport.* Does the instructor demonstrate fair and equitable treatment of the students in the class? Are questions answered in a direct and understandable manner? Does the instructor betray any sarcasm in dealing with students? Does he

72

encourage student involvement when relevant? In dealing with student viewpoints contrary to his own, does the instructor encourage full and fair class discussion? Does he appear receptive to student suggestions? What is the best description of the instructor-student relationship as exhibited in the classroom?

4. *Teaching behaviors.* Is the instructor's oral delivery too rapid, too slow? Can he be easily heard? Is his choice of language understandable to the students? Is the classroom activity level too high, too low? Does the instructor at times express himself nonverbally? Does he exhibit any distracting mannerisms? Does he maintain eye contact with students? Is he blind to any part of the classroom and fail to call on students in that area?

5. *Enthusiastic teaching.* Does the instructor exude enthusiasm for the subject? Does he show signs that he enjoys teaching? How hard does he try to stimulate students to master the subject? Does he encourage informal discussions with students before or after class?

6. *Concern for teaching.* Does the instructor show interest in improving his teaching by an analysis of classroom performance and/or by innovating new teaching techniques? Does the instructor make the subject relevant to students and tie it to recent developments? Does the instructor seek out colleagues for discussions on teaching improvement?

7. *Overall.* What parts of the teaching seemed particularly to enhance the learning process? What suggestions are needed to improve the teaching performance? Does the instructor merit recommendation to students you advise? Was the classroom observation under circumstances that permitted accurate judgment on the efficacy of the teaching-learning process? How would you rate this instructor against others in the department? In the institution?

A few colleges and universities have substituted recording devices in the classroom in place of colleague observation. This substitution has the advantage of being less physically obtrusive but it is highly questionable in that it seems to increase—not lessen—the suspicion and distrust in the faculty. For instance, the presence of a recording device stirs some faculty members to ask: what unannounced use will be made of the recording? Does somebody want to spy on the classroom? Who will control the recording, listen to it? Is the next step to be the policing of the thought-content of the course?

As Eble (1972, p. 61) cautions: "There is a legitimate fear of technology's penchant for violating privacy." Perhaps because of such fear, it is rare for colleges and universities to use audio or videotape recordings in the assessment of teaching performance.

73

Faculty resistance against such use remains strong.

What teaching characteristics do faculty members believe are generally present in the best instructors? In a well-known study, Hildebrand, Wilson and Dienst (1971, pp. 12–14) reported the views of 119 faculty members at the University of California, at Berkeley. The following 25 items are excerpted from the list of such teaching characteristics. The best instructor:

1. Discusses students' work with colleagues
2. Spends much time planning and preparing for his teaching
3. Seems well read beyond the subject he teaches
4. Is sought by colleagues for advice on academic matters
5. Encourages students to talk with him on matters of concern
6. Is involved in campus activities that affect students
7. Meets with students informally out of class
8. Meets with students out of regular office hours
9. Seems to have a congenial relationship with students
10. Seems to have a genuine interest in his students
11. Seeks advice from others about the courses he teaches
12. Discusses teaching in general with colleagues
13. Expresses interest and concern about the quality of his teaching
14. Seems to enjoy teaching and his subject
15. Encourages students to express feelings and opinions
16. Clarifies thinking by identifying reasons for questions
17. Presents facts and concepts from related fields
18. Anticipates difficulties and prepares students beforehand
19. Quickly grasps what a student is asking or telling him
20. Is careful and precise in answering questions
21. Presents origins of ideas and concepts
22. Emphasizes ways of solving problems rather than solutions
23. Invites discussion of points he raises
24. Is conscientious about keeping appointments with students
25. Recognizes and greets students out of class

Key Requirements of a Colleague Evaluation System

In the introduction at colleges and universities of colleague evaluation based, in part, on classroom observation, several considerations are important enough to keep on the front burner.

1. Colleague observation is a component, and only a component, in the system of teacher evaluation. Its aim must be clearly defined and understood by students, faculty and administrators.

2. Faculty resistance is a fact of campus life and can best be met by disarming candor and sympathetic understanding at open forums. Forceful opening of the classroom door to observers will

lead directly to faculty obstructionism and reduced faculty morale. Institutions must prepare the introduction of colleague observation by responding openly and with sincerity to each faculty objection. The institutions must display a sensitivity, patience and a willingness to compromise.

3. There is no substitute for goodwill, mutual trust, respect and support, and both the institutions and faculty must strive for those ends if classroom observation is to be successful.

4. The primary purpose of colleague evaluation is the improvement of teaching and learning.

5. If the information is carefully gathered, promptly reported and judiciously interpreted, colleague evaluation based in part on classroom observation is capable of solid judgments on merit increases, promotion and tenure.

6. Avoid burdening classroom visitation with bureaucratic complexity. Keep the system simple, clear, acceptable to the observing colleague and the teacher he is observing. Train the colleague in what, and how, to observe. Explain the results to the teacher and use them judiciously.

7. If successful, colleague evaluation will result finally in genuine teaching improvement, a profounder understanding of learning psychology, a more effective armory of instruction techniques.

Choosing an Instrument for Colleague Evaluation

Unlike the vast number of available student evaluation forms, relatively few colleague evaluation forms exist. Some institutions have developed checklists on classroom materials, extent of innovation, appropriateness of syllabus, reading lists, fairness of examinations. Together with the instructor's explanation of their uses, such colleague evaluation forms offer some insights into teaching performance.

However, few colleges and universities have developed standardized, research-supported evaluation instruments for use in classroom visitations. This paucity in itself has contributed to the scant use of colleague observation in faculty evaluation systems.

What are the essentials to be included in a colleague observation instrument?

It must include questions specific enough to generate some comparative information. A point-range system (for example, 1–7) is an easy response format. There must be sufficient space for open-end comments. All the intended uses of the instrument must be explicitly stated to erase from the minds of rater and ratee the possibility of additional use.

The instrument must be flexible enough to encompass any special talents or unique contributions to the department or institution. Yet it must be specific enough to focus the observer on all the important teaching areas.

If the instrument calls for appraisal of course-related materials, it must spell out the procedures to be followed for such appraisal. If questions on classroom teaching performance are asked, clear procedures on obtaining reliable answers must be stated.

A few colleges and universities have developed instruments requesting the observer to relate the evidence on which the appraisal rests. Other colleges and universities request the teacher to select from a list those information sources he considers most appropriate to his teaching performance.

As previously underscored in the discussion on student evaluation, the success or failure of the colleague observation program is contingent on the common acceptance by observer and teacher of the appropriateness, reasonableness and fairness of the rating instrument and its implementation. If the observer and/or the teacher have misgivings about any segment of the process it may be foredoomed to partial failure. To steer between the Charybdis of teacher suspicion and resistance and the Scylla of observer mishandling of the instrument is a mighty administrative challenge. It demands sensitizing the participants to the need for the instrument and a readiness to compromise to gain the acceptance of the participants without reservation.

Guidelines for a Successful Colleague Visitation Program

The following guidelines are based on a synthesis of successfully operating programs in colleges and universities. It is suggested that

Form 4.
CLASSROOM OBSERVATION REPORT

Instructor evaluated _____ Course _____

Number of students present _____ Date _____

Evaluator(s) _____

Purpose: The purpose of this classroom observation is (1) to provide a data base for more accurate and equitable decisions on tenure, promotion and merit increase, and (2) to improve faculty performance.

Instructions: Please consider each item carefully and assign the highest scores only for unusually effective performance.

Questions number 12 and 13 have been deliberately left blank. You and the instructor being evaluated are encouraged to add your own items.

Each instructor should be observed on two occasions and the observer(s) should remain in the classroom for the full class period.

It is suggested that the observer(s) arrange a pre-visit and post-visit meeting with the instructor.

Highest		Satisfactory		Lowest	Not Applicable
5	4	3	2	1	n/a

_____ 1. Defines objectives for the class presentation

_____ 2. Effectively organizes learning situations to meet the objectives of the class presentation

_____ 3. Uses instructional methods encouraging relevant student participation in the learning process

_____ 4. Uses class time effectively

_____ 5. Demonstrates enthusiasm for the subject matter

_____ 6. Communicates clearly and effectively to the level of the students

_____ 7. Explains important ideas simply and clearly

_____ 8. Demonstrates command of subject matter

_____ 9. Responds appropriately to student questions and comments

_____10. Encourages critical thinking and analysis

_____11. Considering the previous items, how would you rate this instructor in comparison to others in the department?

_____12.

_____13.

_____14. Overall rating

Would you recommend this instructor to students you are advising. (Please explain.)

What specific suggestions would you make concerning how this particular class could have been improved?

Did you have a pre-visit conference?———Post-visit conference?————

two tenured faculty members be selected as colleague observers. They should be selected by the academic dean in consultation with the department chairman, and each should have the charismatic reputation not only as gifted teacher but also as superior human being. If they lack skills as trained classroom observers, they should receive such training.

The date of the classroom observation should be fixed by mutual agreement between the colleague observers and the teacher. The teacher's preference should be honored when possible. The teacher should brief the observers on the purpose and objectives of the class to be observed, and the instructional modes selected by the teacher to achieve these objectives.

A standardized appraisal form (see examples in Forms 4, 5, 6) should be used and fully explained to the teacher. In a few cases, institutions have modified their student evaluation forms to serve as

Form 5.
CLASSROOM OBSERVATION REPORT

Instructor evaluated _____ Course _____

Number of students present _____ Date _____

Evaluator(s) _____

Purpose: The purpose of this classroom observation report is to provide a point of departure for improving teaching.

Instructions: Several days prior to the classroom visit, the instructor should provide the observer with a copy of the course syllabus containing course objectives, content, and organization as well as the means that will be used to assess student achievement.

The observer should meet with the instructor within 3 days after the visit to discuss his observations and conclusions.

Please feel free to use the reverse side of this page to elaborate on your comments.

1. Describe the instructor's teaching as it relates to content mastery, breadth and depth.

2. Describe the method of instruction.

3. How clear and well-organized is the presentation?

4. Why do you consider the instruction to be of an appropriate or inappropriate level and quality?

5. Describe the form and extent of student participation.

6. What specific suggestions would you make to improve instruction in this particular class?

colleague evaluation forms. In such cases, a useful comparison between student and faculty observations may be obtained.

The two colleagues must remain as an observing team in the classroom for the duration of the class. Each then drafts an individual initial report, preferably on the day of observation but no later than 24 hours. The two reports are then examined line by line to determine similarities and iron out differences. A joint report is prepared and in a few days discussed in detail with the teacher by the colleague observers. The teacher is invited to respond to every step in the joint report. If the report is intended for personnel decisions, it should contain the teacher's written comments before it is handed to the department chairman and dean.

There is another successful approach to colleague observation that is open to colleges and universities. In this approach, each faculty member facing a tenure, promotion in rank, or contract renewal decision, is requested by the academic dean to submit five or six names of colleagues willing to evaluate his instructional performance. The dean selects three of the names. Each of the three is given a standardized classroom observation form. Individually, the three make at least two classroom visitations, as agreed upon by the observer and the teacher.

Each classroom visit is preceded by a conference between observer and teacher, and after the class the two get together for a critical discussion. The teacher is given a copy of the completed evaluation form. He can supplement the evaluation with written comments, insights, criticism which are sent along with the evaluation to the dean.

At Harvard University, the Faculty of Arts and Sciences set up a Task Force on Pedagogical Improvement (1977) which suggested as evidentiary sources of teaching performance (1) examination of course design and innovations in classroom presentation, (2) examination of course material, including syllabi, reading lists, examinations and corrected papers, (3) audiotapes or videotapes on classroom teaching, (4) oral presentations to other department members, (5) direct observation of teaching.

Each academic department has the option of accepting or rejecting any evidence considered inappropriate or immaterial. Each department may develop its own evaluative instrument so long as it provides for general assessment and reliable evidence of performance.

If the faculty member is considered for promotion or tenure, and the department decides to use colleague observation, the Task Force recommends that the faculty member's classroom performance be evaluated on at least two occasions by two senior faculty members, one of whom may be the chairman. Generally, the two observations will be of different classes in different semesters.

As the minimal alternative to classroom observation, the Task Force recommends that several department members listen to and appraise the teacher's speaking at a public forum at Harvard or elsewhere. Traditionally, at Harvard, a candidate for appointment is invited to lecture department members as a screening method.

Form 6.
COLLEAGUE DESCRIPTION OF TEACHERS, SHORT FORM

INSTRUCTOR————————————————————————————

DEPARTMENT————————————————————————————

I. The following items reflect some of the ways teachers can be described. For the instructor named above, please circle the number which indicates the degree to which you feel each item is descriptive of him or her. In some cases, the statement may not apply to this individual. In these cases, check *Does not apply or don't know* for that item.

	Not at all Descriptive	Very Descriptive	Doesn't apply or don't know

1. Does original work that receives serious attention from others, corresponds with others about his work, expresses interest in colleagues' work, gives papers at conferences and keeps up with current developments   1 2 3 4 5 6 7   ( )

2. Is well read in and knowledgeable about his subject and related fields and is sought out by colleagues for advice on academic matters

3. Encourages students to talk with him, is involved in campus activities and has a congenial relationship with colleagues

4. Meets with students informally and is conscientious about appointments and office hours. Recognizes his students and encourages them to talk with him

5. Is interested in teaching, seeks advice and discusses teaching with colleagues

6. Is friendly toward and interested in the work of his colleagues

    (Additional items may be presented by instructor and/or department)

II.

1. How does this instructor compare with other teachers at *this school?*

Among the very worst		About average		Among the very best	
1	2	3	4	5	6	7

2. How does this instructor compare with other teachers in *this department?*

Among the very worst		About average		Among the very best	
1	2	3	4	5	6	7

80

You are invited to comment further on the effectiveness of this instructor especially in areas not covered by the questions.

Source: Developed by Robert C. Wilson and Evelyn R. Dienst, Center for Research and Development in Higher Education, University of California, Berkeley. Form CMF. Reproduced by permission of the authors.

At Harvard Business School, tenured faculty members are directly responsible for coaching and later evaluating the teaching performance of non-tenured faculty. The responsibility of the tenured faculty members extends to classroom visitation to assess progress in teaching improvement. Written reports are periodically submitted to the chairman.

Summary

Colleague evaluation based on the twin analyses of course material and classroom observation is unquestionably an aid in a comprehensive assessment of teaching performance. Colleagues are in a unique position to spot teaching weaknesses and to aid in their correction. If the frame of reference is mutual trust and respect, fairness, and a genuine interest in improvement, colleague evaluations, judiciously interpreted, can also apply to personnel decisions. That is a big if. Relatively few colleges and universities have developed and use reliable instruments for colleague observation. There is widespread faculty resistance, overt and covert, to colleague observation based on its distrust as a reliable method, as an invasion of privacy, and as a damaging potential in the hands of administration.

Any operation bootstrap is inherently difficult but not at all impossible. The fact that some colleges and universities, albeit a few, are successfully using colleague observation for teaching improvement and personnel decisions, suggests that other institutions can also develop among its employees sufficient mutual trust for the colleague evaluation program to work. The rewards to faculty, administration and students are worth the effort.

Chapter 5

Self-Evaluation

Whether faculty self-evaluation is of value as a component in appraising overall teaching performance has long been challenged. Does it add a dimension to such more accepted components as a colleague's review of instructional material? Or classroom visitation? Or student evaluation? Can self-evaluation truly be helpful in tenure, promotion and salary decisions? Most important, can it help to improve teaching?

Literature and Research

Faculty self-evaluation has been accepted as useful by a small number of educators. An early position paper by Simpson and Seidman (1962) accepted it with the caveat that because so little was known about the inside mechanisms of self-evaluation its practical value was lessened. Mayhew (1967) also favored self-evaluation but warned against its use as sole justification for salary increase or promotion in rank. Dressel (1970) supports self-evaluation as essential for an instructor to face up to his teaching weaknesses so as to overcome them.

Eble (1972, p. 62) argues that a good "searching" self-evaluation can lead to "a resolve to improve one's skills." He is also aware of the general low esteem in which self-evaluation is held by faculty members who regard it as superfluous in dealing with professional teachers.

Miller (1974, p. 27) accords self-evaluation "a more prominent place in overall faculty . . . evaluation." In today's age of introspection and heightened interest in human relations and in human psychology, a spinoff benefit is renewed interest in self-evaluation.

Several prominent researchers in Great Britain also support self-evaluation. Bligh (1975, p. 213) advances the position that the appraisal "of one's own teaching in order to improve it should be both the most important and the most frequent kind of assessment." He also believes it should be a consideration in promotion. Further, he believes that teachers should have the option of using "any methods they please . . . but they should be expected to justify their choice."

Support also comes from Sayer and Harding (1975) who urge the substitution of the teacher's personally developed guidelines for the elaborately standardized versions to measure teaching effectiveness. Not only do they urge the teacher to develop his own guidelines but also to produce the evidence of his effective teaching.

All in all, self-evaluation has drawn fire from the faculty in general because of an abiding mistrust of its accuracy and reliability as a meaningful yardstick.

Bayley (1967, p. 115) argues that faculty members apparently believe that only they can "recognize the worth of . . . an individual teacher. . . ." He cautions that this may be, in some cases, tantamount to self-delusion and that the teacher's estimation of himself "can hardly be accepted at face value."

Ozmon (1967) agrees in that he views self-appraisal as an inherently faulty mechanism, since every teacher tends to look on himself as a good teacher. An honest self-appraisal, according to Ozmon, is rare.

Kulik (1974, p. 4) envisions self-evaluation as partly a problem of numbers. Unlike student ratings, for example, self-evaluation is one man's judgment of himself. If he is "dull but generous" he will value his services high; if he is a brilliant but self-effacing teacher he can end up with a poor rating.

Significantly, in the evaluation models developed by Morton (1961), Smart (1965), Megaw (1967) and Hildebrand and Wilson (1970), although self-evaluation is not specifically criticized, it is omitted from each researcher's assessment system.

The research literature on self-evaluation is thin and inconclusive but most studies indicate a yawning chasm between student and colleague evaluations and the teachers' self-evaluations.

One study by Webb and Nolan (1955) found a high correlation between student ratings and instructor self-rating. But this finding is rendered dubious by the flawed technique of using supervisory instructors at the Jacksonville Naval Air Technical Training School instead of college and university faculty.

Sorey (1968) found that superior teachers are more accurate in self-evaluations than mediocre teachers. Choy (1969), using only one overall measure of teaching effectiveness, obtained a modest correlation between self and student rating. This was also the finding by Clark and Blackburn (1971) who came up with modest agreement between self-rating as against the ratings by students, faculty colleagues and administrators.

In a study of over 300 teachers in five colleges, Centra (1972) found more evidence of teacher astigmatism in viewing his own effectiveness as a teacher. In this study the instructor's self-rating on 17 items was correlated with the mean response of students in his class. The median correlation was .21, suggesting only a modest relationship between the two. As might be expected, the highest correlations were on factual items (for example, the instructor informs students how they will be graded) and the lowest were on more subjective items (for example, the instructor uses class time well).

Self-Evaluation for Personnel Decisions

Some institutions use self-evaluation as one component in a multi-component evaluation system. This has the obvious advantage of adding another piece of evidence to the collective judgment. The American Association of University Professors (1974, p. 169) concludes on balance that, despite the limitations, "a contribution to self-evaluating teaching (is made by) giving faculty members the opportunity to assess their own teaching effectiveness and to add their own interpretation of student ratings and classroom visitation."

What, specifically, can an instructor in a self-evaluation contribute that will benefit a multi-source evaluation system? First and foremost, is the intended classroom objectives and the methods used to achieve these objectives. Clear, simple, factual, candid self-appraisals simplify the task of the personnel review committees and administrators to come up with fair judgments of teaching performance.

Mandatory is a standardized format for the information needed.

In some institutions a list of faculty activities ("brag sheets") is solicited for this information. Clearly, this reporting format is entirely too loose, vague, and self-serving to serve two masters. What's more, faculty members are often asked to assess the quality of their own efforts, without the aid of specific, objective criteria. The inevitable result: a gathering of information unreliable for personnel decisions. Unfortunately, this system is a favorite on campuses today.

On the contrary, an instructor's report on himself, to be useful, needs to spell out in specific terms the objectives, activities, accomplishments, failures during the year. What is wanted is less quantity and more quality as clues to performance. Data on teaching, student advising, research and scholarship, community and institutional service are useful clues. Illustrative material and hard evidence of accomplishment are needed.

Centra (1977, p. 95) suggests that the self-report include "the objectives and syllabus of course, the methods and materials used in instruction, assignments and examinations, and, if possible, evidence of student learning, on accomplishments in the course such as course projects, term papers, and pretest and posttest results."

If the data are carefully gathered, using a standardized format, and interpreted judiciously, self-evaluation can be useful to the evaluation process. It offers a basis for colleague, promotion committee, and administrator judgment. But no one should rely on self-evaluation as the sole basis for personnel decision.

Self-Evaluation for Improving Performance

At most colleges and universities self-evaluation is found to be more useful to improve teaching performance than to enter into personnel decision. The importance of offering faculty members the opportunity of a truly searching self-reflection, without fear of retribution no matter what is revealed, can lead to the resolution and the implementation to improve teaching skills.

It has been manifested many times that self-evaluation can have a positive effect on teaching. The reason, as Miller (1972, p. 35) points out, is perhaps that as the instructor develops his self-awareness "he is able to respond more effectively to the needs and interests of others, and he is more likely to observe unspoken clues to behavior and needs."

Despite this estimable benefit, self-analysis in a vacuum holds at best limited promise to improve teaching. Some teachers simply do not know how to evaluate their performance. Others can identify strengths and weaknesses but are at a loss at how to proceed from there. And still others are taken in by their own illusionary images of being superb teachers.

How can self-analysis be harnessed to improved teaching performance? How can students, faculty colleagues, instructional consultants and others offer the kind of constructive help that no instructor can resent and that can hone teaching skills?

In general, the approach is by a sympathetic comparison and discussion of student and self-rating, audio and videotape of teaching behavior in the classroom, and a friendly discussion on teaching with faculty colleagues or teaching consultants.

Student Ratings. The value of having the teacher complete the identical evaluation form completed by his students has been proved at many institutions. In this approach, the evaluation form is given first to the students to complete, then to the teacher. Then the teacher is asked to redo the evaluation form with the ratings he anticipates his students will give him. Thus, the ground is prepared for the teacher's examination of his own estimation of his teaching, his students' estimations, and the accuracy of his perceptions about how his students feel about his classroom teaching. A careful and honest analysis of the triad can be fruitful to the teacher desirous of improvement. Any jarring discrepancy in the three ratings should signal the need for closer scrutiny.

Confronted by such discrepancy, some instructors find it helpful to spend part of a class period in open discussion with the students. "This procedure has some drawbacks," as Miller (1974, p. 28) suggests, "and it would not fit some instructors' personalities, but it has been used effectively."

The question remains, will an instructor's performance improve after his cognizance that his students take a much dimmer view of his teaching than he does? Pambookin (1977) says yes, especially if the teacher's self-rating is far apart from the students' ratings, favorable or unfavorable. Pambookin also finds that student ratings sharply less favorable than the instructor's self-rating are more likely to lead to teaching improvement than the reverse.

Although a more negative student appraisal than the instructor's self-appraisal prepares the climate for change, not all instructors know how to effect the change. Kansas State University has a useful approach.

Its program rests on the assumption that there are different effective teaching styles, dependent on the teacher's goals, the nature of the course, the students' characteristics. First, the instructor ranks the importance of eight learning objectives. Second, the students rate their progress in the eight objectives and describe the instructor's classroom behavior. Participating faculty members then receive the ratings and compare them with the average scores of other instructors with similar objectives in similar fields with similar-sized classes.

Thereafter, seminars on educational improvement are open to the instructor who is also encouraged to consult with instructional improvement specialists. At Kansas State University student ratings thus are part of a continuous follow-up teaching improvement program.

Audio and Videotape Feedback. Sensitizing an instructor to his teaching strengths and weaknesses is also helped by audio and videotaped classes. Most people have selective memories, and teachers are no exceptions. They tend to recall classroom highlights and an audio and videotaped class can fill in important but forgotten details. Replays of teaching behavior help point up teaching strengths and weaknesses. The replays can be analyzed by the classroom students, faculty colleagues, or instructional improvement specialists. One caution should be observed. Since viewing one's self-teaching in a classroom for the first time on tape may be rather traumatic, it is urged that the instructor be the first to see himself on camera. Later viewings by others can then be focused more fruitfully on specifics of the camera record.

Some teachers are capable of listening and viewing a videotaped record of their classes and at once—working alone—can recognize how to improve their teaching. But most teachers require others to help analyze and suggest modifications in particular practices and teaching behaviors.

Rezler and Anderson (1971) report that teachers who view videotapes of their classes as part of a group failed to change their preconceptions of themselves as teachers unless the replay was stopped at selected incidents and the teachers' attentions were directed to specific teaching behaviors.

The use of tapes to improve instruction is hardly restricted to U.S. colleges and universities. At the Swiss Federal Institute of Technology (Lausanne), for example, all faculty members have a standing invitation to have their classes videotaped. By using two and more cameras, the teaching and the student reaction can be simultaneously recorded. At the instructor's option, the videotape can be viewed privately, with his students, or with faculty colleagues and/or instructional improvement specialist.

An unusual and important feature of the Institute program is that each instructor is provided with a checklist to help identify and assess aspects of his teaching. Periodically, with the instructor's approval, seminars are held using a split screen on which tape excerpts of teacher and students are shown and candidly discussed.

Discussions on Teaching. Some researchers are persuaded that improved teaching is dependent not only on cognitive knowledge and skills but also on the personal make-up of the teacher. To change his personal make-up, and thereby improve his teaching, he must be made to confront his most cherished (and unchallenged) assumptions, values and attitudes. In the process of clarifying his teaching attitude, for example, improved performance may result.

The trouble is, this is not always achievable. Many faculty members are reticent about discussing their attitude on teaching. Several reasons have been offered by Berquist and Phillips (1975).

(1) Faculty members tend to view themselves in a particular discipline rather than in the teaching profession. (2) The tradition of classroom autonomy leaves almost no room for a discussion of teaching. (3) Since most faculty members enter teaching without benefit of formal training they tend to shrink from articulating their rationale for teaching. (4) When faculty members engage in committee work almost no time is spent on teaching/learning issues. (5) Most faculty members do not really understand and therefore do not support team-teaching in higher education.

One method of meeting these problems is the in-depth interview in which the teacher is asked probing questions about his teaching. The purpose is to sensitize the teacher about himself as a teacher. Such interview routinely runs one to three hours and is conducted by a trained faculty member.

Sanford (1971) sees an advantage in recruiting the interviewer from outside the department and even the institution. In that case, the interviewer offers no competitive threat and projects a more objective image. Unfortunately, the cost of an outside interviewer is prohibitive for many institutions.

Typically, the interview includes such questions as:
1. "Where did you do your graduate work?"
2. "How did you decide to become a teacher?"
3. "What do you enjoy most about teaching? Least?"
4. "How effective are you as a teacher?"
5. "If you were not a teacher, what would you like to be?"
6. "What is the one criticism that you are most fearful of receiving from a student? From a colleague?"
7. "If this were your last term teaching, would you do anything different? What?"
8. "What is your greatest strength as a teacher? Weakness?"
9. "What do you consider your greatest accomplishment as a teacher in the last three years? Your greatest failure?"
10. "What is the most important thing a student can learn from you?"

Instead of a two-person interview, at times a small faculty group is assembled and asked to reflect on each question and enter a group discussion on each answer. The value of group discussion is the dilution of personal misgivings about revealing innermost thoughts and concerns about teaching. Each participant learns that his colleagues share his doubts and qualms. By sharing, each emerges from the group discussion more self-aware, more knowledgeable, and more self-confident as a teacher.

Such faculty discussions need not be limited to individual teaching beliefs and values. The discussions can profitably include teaching problems, reading lists, course objectives, student assignments. Even the results of class examinations can be shared with colleagues. It may be discovered that students in many classes are deficient in common areas, which can underline the need to review the subject by all the teachers.

Administration's Role in Self-Evaluation to Improve Teaching

There is no question that self-evaluation, aided immeasurably by student ratings, classroom visitations, and instructional improvement specialists can and does improve teaching performance. There is also no question that the administration's role during this process is vital. It can largely aid or destroy the process. It must foster and support the environment necessary to encourage teachers to improve their classroom performance. By its actions, the administration must dispel any suspicion that a revealed teaching weakness will be held against the teacher and turn up some time to his professional disadvantage. In the absence of complete confidence in the administration, the teaching staff cannot be expected to participate unconditionally in teaching improvement programs.

How is this complete trust to be won? As a starter, Berquist and Phillips (1975) suggest that communications between administration and faculty flow freer and frequently. Where possible, status differences, such as self-evaluation only of non-tenured teachers, should be reduced or eliminated. Good-teaching awards should be developed as well as team-building activities at the department level. The faculty interview should have as one objective the nurturing of trust and truthfulness as a campus norm. An initial step can be to interview the department chairman and, with his assent, to discuss his responses with faculty members.

Problems in Self-Evaluation

Each teacher routinely, if informally, evaluates his classroom performance by observing its effect on the students. But this observation may be limited. As McKeachie (1978, p. 275) suggests, "few teachers can ignore students who are sleeping or reading newspapers." But many teachers fail to notice "restless shifting of position, blank stares, whispered asides, and other indications that students are not with them."

Some teachers approach self-evaluation by the use of student questionnaires. Their attempts at self-evaluation merit encouragement. But the results are often robbed of value because the questions are not specific and the responses are neither objective nor comprehensive. Also, self-assessment is often conducted at the end of the semester so that needed teaching modifications are of no benefit to that class.

At some institutions, the self-evaluation techniques are imposed on the teacher by the department chairman or academic dean. This produces in many teachers an undesirable side-effect of anxiety which almost inevitably contaminates the techniques.

Some teachers are persuaded that self-evaluation can be tolerated as a one-shot activity. But without a continuing program of self-evaluations there is no possible way to measure improvement.

Some teachers find it convenient to infer answers to self-evaluation questions from their students' classroom performance. For example, in answer to the question, "Are class presentations well planned and organized?"—they will reply without asking students or colleagues for their views.

Guiding Questions for Self-Evaluation

It is a truism that self-evaluation by itself can guarantee neither teaching improvement nor usable information about a teacher's performance. But the likelihood of obtaining either or both is increased with the careful development of the self-evaluation process and the judicious interpretation of its results.

Experience suggests the wisdom of allowing the teacher, who is developing a program of teaching objectives and teaching activities, to write his answers to direct, open-ended, written questions. This format gives the teacher the opportunity to explain in detail the objectives, strategies, and circumstances of his classroom performance.

When completing the self-evaluation forms, the teacher should be cautioned against false modesty about his teaching performance, and against concealing his weaknesses. It is useful to remind the teacher that all practitioners in education, even in the same discipline, have varying concentrations of knowledge in the field and varying familiarity with teaching approaches.

An excellent guide to questions for self-evaluation is Berquist and Phillips (1975). It asks some of the following questions.

Broad teaching skills. Within your discipline, which area do you regard as your strongest? Weakest? Which teaching method do you use most effectively? How do you develop critical thinking skills in your students? How do you explain difficult concepts? How do you stimulate student curiosity? What kind of activities take place in your classroom? Why? Overall, how do you rate your teaching performance in the past year? How does it compare with three years ago? Why?

Course organization and planning. How effectively do you use class time? How do you develop presentations so they are well-planned and organized? When did you last revise your approach to a particular course? Why? Do you change methods to meet new classroom situations? Can you give a recent example? What is the one thing you most want your students to learn?

Feedback to students. How do you inform students of their performance? Do you praise students in front of others? Criticize them? In what ways do you review tests and assignments with students? How important are grades?

Instructor—student rapport. How would you describe the feeling between you and your students? How would you describe the atmosphere in your classroom? In what ways do you encourage relevant student involvement in the class? How do you encourage students to seek your help when necessary? Do students feel you are tolerant of their views if they are different from yours? What kind of student do you most enjoy teaching? What kind of student bothers you?

Knowledge of discipline. How would you judge your content mastery in the courses you presently teach? In what ways have you tried to stay current in your field? How would your faculty colleagues appraise your knowledge of your discipline? If you were to teach another subject, what would it be?

General. What is the best thing that could happen to you in a class? Worst? How do you feel about having some of your colleagues visit your classes? Are there one or two members of the faculty with whom you are likely to discuss your classroom successes? Your failures? What is the one thing you would most like to change about your teaching? Have you taken any steps to bring this change about?

Personal beliefs about teaching. What are the five most important things new teachers in your discipline should know to be effective instructors? What are the five most important things they should be able to do? How would you describe your attitude toward teaching? Has it changed in recent years? In what ways? How do you feel about the amount of influence you have on your students? To what extent do you design your courses to minimize or maximize this influence? Ten years from now, what would you most like your students to remember about you as a teacher? Why?

Another approach to self-evaluation has been developed by Skipper (1975). His technique requires the teacher to complete twenty statements on teaching. For example, "My skill as a teacher is best expressed when I. . . ." Or, "I'm the kind of teacher my colleagues would describe as. . . ." Or, "The most satisfying aspect of teaching is. . . ."

Skipper also suggests several approaches to data analysis and interpretation. In one approach the teacher is asked to group his responses according to different aspects of teaching (for example, instructional skills, or rapport with students). In another approach two separate lists are prepared, of "Five Things I Need to Do to Improve My Teaching," and "The Five Things I Do Best as a Teacher." Still another approach is to ask the teacher to itemize his teaching behavior and skills that might encourage greater interest by students in the subject, and conversely to itemize such behavior and skills that might dampen student interest in the subject.

The incomplete sentence technique of self-evaluation is both novel and promising. To match actual performance with the teacher's written answers could readily be achieved by videotaping several of the teacher's classes. Less effective, but as an alternative, the teacher might ask his students for their perceptions of his responses.

91

USING A SELF-EVALUATION INSTRUMENT

To develop meaningful information, a self-evaluation must be so structured as to elicit the specific data needed. To hand the teacher a sheet of white paper on which he is to evaluate himself is a method most likely to produce worthless information.

Also, it must be kept in mind that self-evaluation is used for two

Form 7.
FACULTY SELF-EVALUATION REPORT
(1979–1980 academic year)

Name _____ Dept. _____ Date _____

PLEASE NOTE: This self-evaluation report should be based only on performance as a faculty member during the 1979–1980 academic year.

Directions: *In rating yourself on each item, please reserve the highest score for unusually effective performance.*

If more space is needed for questions 9, 10, 11, or 12, please use reverse side of page.

Highest		Average		Lowest	Not Applicable
5	4	3	2	1	n/a

_____ 1. Have the major objectives of your course been made clear?

_____ 2. Are class presentations well-planned and organized?

_____ 3. Are difficult topics explained clearly?

_____ 4. Do your students feel free to express ideas and disagree with you?

_____ 5. Are you fair and impartial in dealing with students?

_____ 6. Do you encourage students to seek your help when necessary?

_____ 7. How would you judge your mastery of the content in your courses?

_____ 8. Do you permit outside activities to interfere with your responsibilities as a teacher?

_____ 9. Compared to others in your department, how would you rate your teaching performance?
(Please elaborate)

_____10. Compared to others in your department, how would you rate your research and publication endeavors?
(Please elaborate)

_____11. Compared to others in your department, how would you rate your contribution to college service?
(Please elaborate)

_____12. Considering the previous 11 items, how would you rate your overall performance as a faculty member in this department? (Please elaborate)

purposes each best served by a different instrument.

For administrative decisions on promotion, salary and tenure, the self-evaluation forms should contain general and summary items and be judgmental in character. They should point up the comparative effectiveness of the faculty members. For teaching improvement, the forms should focus on specific and detailed diagnostic questions. Regrettably, many self-evaluation instruments seek to serve both diverse purposes and succeed in falling short of both.

The standardized forms will produce answers to questions such as: (1) Is the instructor's self-evaluation consistent with information

Form 8.

FACULTY SELF-EVALUATION REPORT
(1979–1980 academic year)

Name _____ Dept. _____ Date _____

PLEASE NOTE: This self-evaluation report has been devised to facilitate the process of up-grading professional effectiveness.

Please do not let modesty prevent you from being explicit about your assets. Equally important, try to be just as candid about your shortcomings.

1. Within your discipline, which area do you regard as your strongest?

2. Which area do you regard as your weakest?

3. What is your greatest strength as a teacher?

4. What is the one thing you would most like to change about your teaching?

5. What has been your most significant accomplishment as a faculty member over the past three years?

6. What has been your greatest shortcoming as a faculty member over the past three years?

7. Considering the previous 6 items, how would you rate your overall performance as a faculty member in this department?

93

from other sources? (2) Does the self-evaluation reflect the same weaknesses that turn up in other assessment forms? (3) Does the self-evaluation offer adequate explanation of contradictory information obtained elsewhere? Forms 7 and 8 are typical of those currently in use.

Thus far, no studies have been able to correlate items on self-evaluation forms to the teacher's classroom effectiveness.

At many institutions self-evaluation has become an annual updating of faculty teaching, research, publication and institutional service. Form 9 is a typical activity list. It is urgent that the activity list be complete and accurate, for an omission, no matter how incidental, tends to weaken the faculty's faith and support for the program. Also, it is important to allow the teacher to explain his priorities in pursuing certain areas over others.

Form 9.

FACULTY ACTIVITY REPORT

(1979–1980 academic year)

Name _____ Dept. _____ Date _____

PLEASE NOTE: Your report should include only those activities that took place during the 1979–1980 academic year.

1. *Teaching:* Please list courses taught this year by catalog number, section and number of students.

2. *Research:* Sponsored research (Indicate granting agency and amount).

Other research activity.

3. *Publications:* (Please give publication date and, if a journal, the volume).

4. *Administrative Duties:* (e.g. chairman, program director, etc.)

5. *Committee Work:*

6. *Other College Service:*

7. *Significant Community and Professional Service:* (e.g. school board member, journal editor, officer in a professional society, etc.)

The self-evaluation instrument shares some of the problems of student and colleague evaluation instruments. Getting the teacher involved in selecting the forms and perhaps adding questions of his own will tend to increase his receptivity to the evaluation program and his faith in its validity.

If the self-evaluation forms are also the ones used by students, colleagues and administrators, a comparison of the teacher's estimation with the others can be quite revealing. This does not preclude adding questions to the standardized forms to cover special situations.

In some cases, self-evaluation forms call for an itemization of goals so that a subsequent self-evaluation can be scrutinized for their achievement. This approach offers the advantage of faculty accountability. This can be useful to administrators in personnel decisions.

Self-evaluation, although generally frowned on by faculty members, has a future, especially if it escapes abuses.

Chapter 6

Student Learning

Some academics contend that how much, and how well, a student learns is the best measure of teaching effectiveness. Some go further and argue that student learning is also the only legitimate measure of teaching effectiveness; all other attempts at measuring this effectiveness are flawed. In general, however, it is the position of this group that student achievement should be the single dominant yardstick in judging teaching effectiveness. It follows naturally from this position that poor student achievement signifies poor teaching.

Literature and Research

The literature on the measurement of student learning, whether for teaching improvement or for faculty comparison with an eye to personnel decisions, can be charitably described as meager and inconclusive. Cohen and Brawer (1969) regard student achievement as the acid test of faculty performance. Alexander, Elsom, Means and Means (1971) studied the effect on student achievement of personal interactions with the students which were initiated by the teacher. In the experimental class, the teacher deliberately learned and used the students' names, and opened conversations in the hall with them before and after class. The result: they scored significantly higher in class tests.

In a comprehensive review of over 1000 studies of teacher effectiveness in higher education, Trent and Cohen (1973) could uncover no more than twenty which recognized student achievement as the dominant index of faculty performance. The American Association of University Professors in a "Statement on Teaching Evaluation" (1974, p. 167), accepts as "the most valid measure" the assessment of teacher effectiveness on the basis of student learning, but hastens to add that it is "probably the most difficult to obtain."

Duncan and Biddle (1974) suggest that good teaching can be justifiably so labeled when it is demonstrated that it is chain-linked with student learning. An opposing position is voiced by McKeachie and Kulik (1975) who deflate the enthusiasm for evaluating teachers by student achievement by pointing out the scarcity of data supporting performance yardsticks. They cite practical difficulties, such as the absence of adequate norms, in making student achievement the basis for faculty comparison.

Scott (1975) suggests that facts on student learning can affect professorial function in three important ways: (1) Teaching faculty can use the facts in evaluating both their classroom materials and their teaching innovations; (2) The faculty can apply them when dealing with administrators in matters of self-development or promotion in rank; (3) The teachers can refer to them in their deliberations on course content and objectives or instructional objectives.

Good teaching in a college or university, Starr asserts (1978), cannot be considered apart from student learning. Tuckman (1978, p. 1197) supports this view by urging that "the study of teaching effectiveness on the university campus...should focus...on learning outcomes of students."

Connecting Student Learning and Teaching Effectiveness

The connection is not an obvious one. Due to the wide range in student abilities, it is an overwhelming task to try to pin down teacher effectiveness to what or how much any student learns. It is indeed possible to say that modest learning by average students may reflect teaching prowess superior to greater learning achievement by gifted students. How is a gain of 15 points per student in an average class to be compared with 25 points per student in a gifted class? Which teacher was more effective? The problem is a treacherous cul-de-sac.

Learning at times is only indirectly the result of teaching. If an intensive English Honors course in literary criticism, for example, results in some students having their work published in prestigious literary journals, it is unquestionably a credit to the teacher, but how much credit? How much is due to the institution for developing the program and admitting only the most able students to it? How is something patently indivisible to be divided among teacher, institution and student, to say nothing of the host of individuals and factors that helped produce the ultimate achievement?

To cite another example, if most students studying American history in an urban university with open admissions earn scores markedly lower than the national mean on the Graduate Record Examination, who or what is responsible? The instructor? The students? The open admissions program? The city government which mandated the system in a trade for budgetary support? At whom does the accusing finger point for slow-learning students? It will take a latter-day Solomon to decide.

In spite of, and because of, the ambiguities in assigning credit and blame, an acceptable definition of effective teaching is of vital importance. Donald and Shore (1977, p. 45) make a try at it with this definition:

> It results in, enhances or aids successful learning, directly or indirectly. The combination, indeed integration, of the individual teaching efforts of instructors and the intentional support of a positive learning climate by an institution should create the most favourable circumstances for everyone, especially the students. This integration is at the heart of any systematic approach to teaching in higher education.

Measuring Student Learning

Wide-ranging techniques for obtaining a fix on student learning are suggested in the literature. They can be generally divided into two classes of measurements, direct and indirect.

DIRECT MEASURES OF STUDENT LEARNING

At first glance, it would appear that examination scores or course grades are obvious ways to measure student learning: the higher the grade, the greater the learning. But even cursory thought makes clear this is a flawed approach.

First, although it is conceded that student achievement is influenced by an effective teacher, by no means is the teacher the only influence. Other influences are:

(1) The student's general academic ability and intelligence.
(2) The student's study habits.
(3) Motivation to learn.
(4) Writing ability on essay exams.
(5) Ability to show knowledge on multiple choice exams.
(6) Subjective image of the student in the teacher's mind, favorable or unfavorable.

Each influence can bend or skew student achievement.

Second, many achievement tests do not lend themselves to tying certain teaching characteristics to student learning. For example, if an appraisal of a teacher's ability to develop critical thinking in students is sought, a true-false test would be an inappropriate way to find out. To test whether teacher characteristics are learning-connected requires appropriate examination questions. What are appropriate questions, how are they recognized and constructed? These are very big questions.

To add to the confusion, examination scores are a measure of what students have retained, not necessarily what they have learned. True, a low test score may reflect inadequate learning, but it may also be no more than a reflection of the student's inability to articulate the full level of learning. Or the particular test may not be the best vehicle for the student to demonstrate learning.

The student may have:
(1) Problems in retrieval of information from memory.
(2) Poor motivation.
(3) Difficulty in understanding the question.
(4) Insufficient time.
(5) To cope with distractions during the test.
(6) Pressing problems at home.
(7) A feeling of fatigue or illness.
(8) A "block" during the exam.
(9) Problems with this particular exam.

Some academics believe that the best judge of a teacher's effectiveness is to measure student achievement before and after the course. They urge giving students a multiple-choice pretest on the more important concepts in the course, or a pretest of general knowledge on the subject, even a pretest of the course's final examination.

A major problem in the pretest/posttest approach is that the posttest student performance is likely to be directly influenced by the pretest since the tests are identical. In an effort to duck this problem, psychometricians recently developed a technique known as matrix item sampling. By way of explanation, Scott (1975, p. 68) advises that the technique "can be used to collect student learning data once a faculty member decides that a particular classroom activity can be used to obtain information about *items* rather than information about *students*."

Routine course questions are used to gather data on student learning under matrix item sampling. During the first week of class, the teacher gives each student a mini-test (pretest) which contains questions designed to fix the student's learning level. Although all students are tested, they are given varying questions on the same topic. And no student is asked more than a fraction of the total number of questions. On the final examination (posttest) each student is asked a different set of questions from the ones he answered on the pretest.

Matrix item sampling thus has the potential of producing pretest and posttest data of sufficient merit as to determine a student's learning level. Whether that potential can be realized remains to be seen. At this early stage of development, the technique is in need of further refinement and field-testing. Among its drawbacks, the technique requires extensive testing to assure the same degree of difficulty in all the pretests. There is also the matter of teacher capability in covering all the course material with equal competence. Some students will benefit from the teacher's extra skill and interest in certain topic areas, a benefit that will translate into higher grades on the posttest. Conversely, other students receiving a set of questions in areas less adequately covered by the teacher, will find themselves with less favorable grades. Lastly, the administration of pretests and posttests to a large student body, and making certain that no student receives the same questions on the two tests, can be cumbersome and trying.

Another approach to quantifying learning growth is the edumetric test, which purportedly measures student learning and not brainpower. An edumetric test is constructed of questions that most students answer incorrectly before taking the course and correctly on the final examination. The more students who answer incorrectly, the more qualified the question is for the edumetric test.

Rodin (1975, p. 58-59) is bemused by the test:

Since test items passed only by the brighter students are edumetrically invalid, a natural consequence of adapting edumetric tests would be that material for which edumetrically valid items could not be written would not be taught.

(Since) the student's ability to answer (test items) depends on characteristics such as fluency, I.Q., and sensitivity, which have nothing to do with classroom learning...only by trivializing the questions can the instructor make his test independent of ability. If he does this, more students will do well and he will thereby earn a higher score on the accountability measure.

Even when different sections of the same course are compared, there is a problem in using student achievement as a measure of teacher effectiveness. But when students in different sections are taught by different teachers, the problem is compounded.

Bendig (1953) studied the relationship between student ratings and student achievement. For each student in the introductory psychology classes of five instructors, he obtained an achievement score based on three examinations; he also obtained the students' rating of the course and the instructor. Bendig reported substantial differences in ratings of the course and the five instructors, but trivial differences in student achievement.

Bendig's findings of no real achievement differences in multiple section courses is supported by Dubin and Taveggia (1968, p. 35), who reanalyzed almost 100 studies comparing college teaching and conclude that the "data demonstrate clearly and unequivocally that there is no measurable difference...(between different class sections) when evaluated by student performance on final examinations."

McKeachie and Kulik (1975) speculate that when the same textbook is used in a multiple section course, achievement differences tend to be submerged by the textbook regardless of differences in teaching methods and skills.

Nevertheless, if multiple section courses are used as experimental sites for different teaching methods, it is advisable to assign students to sections randomly, to neutralize intelligence and motivation. And a uniform examination should be given to all sections, one that is not prepared by any of the teachers of the sections, to avoid the possibility of gearing the teaching to the test. Lastly, all the course instructors must come to prior agreement on the common content of the course.

Behavioral objectives. Many academics believe that a true measure of teaching effectiveness is how well the students achieve instructional or behavioral objectives. These objectives describe learning goals and are divided into three broad categories (Tuckman, 1978). The first category: the content goal. This refers to the accumulation of facts, concepts, theories and procedures that the instructor plans to transmit to the students. A course outline is made up of content goals. The second category is the process goal. This refers to learning how to conduct independent research, using inductive and deductive reasoning. Learning to think like an anthropologist, historian or economist is a process goal. The third category is the transfer goal. This refers to what affects students outside the classroom, for example in personal and career development.

Instructors who want to hitch their teaching effectiveness to student achievement must initially generate a list of learner outcomes which must not overlook any of the three categories. And the learner outcomes have to be articulated in specific and measurable terms, for example using such action verbs as contrast, arrange, or define. For additional information on the writing of behavioral objectives, see Mager (1978).

Undoubtedly, the use of behavioral objectives has promise as a way to measure teacher effectiveness but the approach is constrained by three problems.

First, instructors rarely specify what they want students to accomplish in the class; even when they do, it is in general language devoid of clear, relevant, measurable terms. Words whose precise meaning is difficult to pin down like "understanding" and

101

"appreciation" are favorite ambiguities. They are of no help in the development of measures to indicate how close students have come to achieve the behavioral objectives.

Second, even when properly written, behavioral objectives apply only to a part of teaching. Factors beyond course materials and the classroom teaching have a bearing on student achievement. As Eble (1972, p. 63) has suggested, "the teacher may become relatively less important as a performer and more important as a designer of learning devices." However, it is still necessary in teacher evaluation to perceive how the teacher's performance in the classroom advances student learning.

Third, the use of behavioral objectives is largely restricted to colleges and universities which emphasize the latest approaches to teaching such as individual instruction, competency-based instruction and contract learning. Most institutions still pursue the traditional approaches to teaching. The result is that information on student learning as indicated by the achievement of behavioral objectives is rare.

Criterion-referenced testing. An important factor in measuring learning via behavioral objectives is the method of determining what has been learned, the evaluation procedure itself. Once behavioral objectives are fixed, the minimum level of student performance in meeting these objectives is decided. Evaluation of learning can presumably then be based on what the student learns rather than on a comparison with his peers. This is called criterion-referenced testing. Its proponents point to the elimination of some of the fuzziness in evaluation that comes up like crabgrass with each year's changes in the average ability of the class. Further, they are sanguine about improved teaching as a result of the criterion-referenced testing approach.

Rose (1976, p. 11) concedes that the procedure may initially be difficult but she argues that the payoff from criterion-referenced testing is worth the effort:

> By defining specific objectives before instruction, teachers will more likely use relevant instructional materials to help students attain the objectives. The process of defining objectives requires instructors to think through exactly what they want to teach, and they are then more likely to aim for truly worthwhile goals. Also, students' progress can be improved while the course is in progress, not after the fact.

What are the pitfalls? What are the hazards in gauging teaching effectiveness by student achievement of behavioral objectives, and as measured by criterion-referenced testing?

To begin with, some faculty members may not be as effective as their students' performance suggests. If an institution were to grant tenure and appropriate salary to the top students completing a teacher's course, it would probably have on its staff many instructors who formulate low-level objectives, or teach students only how to achieve good grades. Many of these teachers would place highest value on student test scores so as to safeguard their own professional futures.

Further, criterion-referenced testing demands the expertise that is the end product of time-consuming and expensive educational training in the proper formulation of behavioral objectives and the construction of criterion-referenced tests.

Thus, although the combination of behavioral objectives and criterion-referenced tests holds promise as a direct measure of student learning, it is not yet reliable enough for faculty decisions on tenure, promotion or salary.

INDIRECT MEASURES OF STUDENT LEARNING

Although direct measures of student learning as a reflection of teacher effectiveness predominate in the literature, several indirect measures have also been suggested.

One is the observance of student progress in subsequent courses in the same discipline as an indicator of the quality of the prior learning experience. As observers, all the professors in this discipline are in a judgmental position of each other.

Another is the establishment of a feedback system in the course so that improvements may be made. Teachers can ask interested students for their perceptions of the learning process, or through student response cards or rating forms obtain feedback on the teaching/learning process.

Still another is the Student Learning Scales (SLS) now being developed at the University of Nebraska. SLS is designed to focus attention on learners rather than on instructors. Because of the scant research on student learning reactions themselves, the researchers have employed many educational theories and models (for example, Bloom, Gagne, and operant learning) to generate items describing valued learning reactions. The items are written in the first person and students are asked for a graded response which describes their learning experience in a particular class. Examples of items: (1) "I was able to use course materials and experiences to improve my problem-solving and decision-making skills." (2) "I was able to function as an independent learner in this class." Although in the early stages of development, the University of Nebraska researchers seem confident after administering the 51-item SLS to

179 students of the practicality of measuring student learning reactions (UN News, 1978).

And still another approach is the survey technique. Widely employed is the exit interview containing scaled items requiring answers according to a predetermined response mode. Student testimonials represent another survey technique used in the indirect assessment of student learning. It offers the advantage of eliminating the possible interviewer bias inherent in the exit interview. Both of these survey approaches suffer from a common flaw: the data are unsystematically collected and thus it is impossible to categorize and quantify the responses.

Donald and Shore (1977) suggest six additional indices of student learning: (1) A frequency count of student requests for further information about topics mentioned in class; (2) The extent of interaction sought by students with their instructor out of class; (3) The use by students of bibliographies and suggested readings in the subject; (4) The level of student attendance, lateness, participation in optional class sessions, drop-out rate; (5) Additional elective courses in the same discipline chosen by the students; and (6) The number pursuing graduate work or considering teaching careers in the same subject.

While these indirect measures may offer useful clues to student learning, more substantive evidence is required for a reasonably accurate appraisal of teaching effectiveness.

Claiming Credit for Student Learning

Clearly, the evaluation of teaching is highly resistant to objective examination. Thus stake claims on credit for student learning are profuse and easy to make. Any instructor can claim responsibility for student achievements without the hard proof demanded in scientific tests. Conversely, any instructor can disclaim responsibility for inadequate student learning. The core problem is that teaching and learning are extraordinarily difficult, if not impossible, to isolate. Disputes are rampant even about the weight properly to be accorded to classroom teaching when student learning can be demonstrated. As Eble (1972, p. 63) points out, "Within the institutional context, the forces that bear upon a student's learning in any class are probably as wide as his range of activities and thoughts during the quarter."

Nevertheless, in the face of overwhelming challenge, some academics persist in the view that the instructor is totally responsible for student achievement. It would appear at the very least that courtesy dictates sharing the credit with the student since the learning takes place within him. Sharing is more generous to the instructor than some researchers are willing to go. They argue that students are not taught by the instructors in any direct sense. Grasha (1977, p. 21) accepts a more moderate position: he views the teacher as "a manager of and one of several resources in a learning environment." Most academics should find this moderate position more comfortable.

Among the "several" classroom resources are the instructor, course outlines, readings, reference lists, lecture notes, textbooks, handouts, syllabi, non-reading assignments, term papers, examinations, field trips, audio-visual aids. Effectively managed by the instructor these resources promote student learning. Credit for the end product—learning—can be awarded in modest degree to the instructor. How much is open to hot argument.

How much a student grows and develops is also a consequence of factors beyond the instructor's control. Today higher education is no longer reserved for the intellectual elite, and there are wide-ranging differences among students in their capacity to learn. There are gifted and slow-learners among them. They are harassed by a panoply of problems involving roommates, boy friend/girl friend, money, career, tensions at home, to list a few. Is the instructor at fault if a student grapples unsuccessfully with problems and fails to learn? Is the instructor to be held responsible for low intellectual capacity?

Student Learning and Teaching Improvement

Regrettably, most teachers follow the practice of assessing student learning when they award grades, and not before. And many neglect to use the results of examinations to promote individual student learning. Today a number of colleges and universities are adopting a mastery learning approach—such as the Keller plan—which provides each student with feedback on performance for each unit of the course. Students proceed at an individual pace and advance to the next segment only after mastering the preceding units. The process is in effect a periodic student assessment and yields benefits to students and teacher.

Some teachers find it useful at times to review the notes taken in class by students. If the review includes students of varying capacity the teachers will soon learn which students do and don't grasp the course essentials, and changes in instruction can accordingly be made.

Other teachers find the short quiz, announced at the opening of class, of estimable value in learning how completely the students understand a special lecture or presentation. Gaps in student understanding can then be filled in by the teacher.

The responses to every question on the quiz should be scrutinized for clues to student understanding. Did most students do well in

105

general but poorly on particular questions? Did most students find the exam too difficult? This may suggest that the content is too difficult or the pace too fast. Did gifted students perform up to their usual high level? If not, the content and instructional methodology may need revising.

An appraisal of student learning for the purpose of improving instruction is generally not seen in a threatening light by faculty members. Thus, gaining their support poses no problems. The real problem resides in the fact that few teachers know how to use the data generated by student learning indices to improve their teaching. They are willing but unknowledgeable in this area.

Improved teaching is more likely from a review of student learning data if the teacher invites peer assistance, especially in departments such as educational psychology where a high order of expertise in testing and measurement can be found. In addition, there is the Center for Teaching Improvement operating today on many college and university campuses, where specialists are available to interpret and help correct teaching defects. The Center for Teaching Improvement is known by other names. On some campuses it is called the Center for Faculty Development, Teaching/Learning Center, or Center for Teaching Resources.

Student Learning and Faculty Personnel Decisions

When a faculty member applies for promotion in rank or tenure, he normally prepares a summary of accomplishments in teaching, research and service. Appended to the application often are copies of published articles, student or peer evaluations, and laudatory correspondence. Rarely in the package of supportive evidence is there any mention, much less documentation, on student learning in his classes. This omission in faculty applications has an unbroken tradition of hundreds of years behind it.

The reason? Simply that the multitude of influences on student achievement render it incapable of being used to compare teachers in different disciplines, or in different courses in the same discipline.

Ample research demonstrates that measures of student learning will reveal nothing but statistically insignificant differences in student achievement in multiple sections of the same course. Another obstacle against the use of student learning data in multiple sections of the same course is the lack of random distribution of student capacity and motivation in the multiple sections. Students habitually select course sections because of favorable scheduling, friendships, and teacher preferences. It is patently improper to base faculty personnel decisions on student achievement in different sections. To do so would institutionalize invalid personnel decisions to say nothing of the professional havoc it would sow among the faculty.

Placing Student Learning in Perspective

If information about student learning is used by the instructor only for the purpose of improving teaching, it can claim some redeeming value. Despite its crippling limitations, the instructor can use the information in the narrow area of class content, methodology and materials. Even in this narrow area, he must in the interest of accuracy supplement his information with student and peer ratings, and any other relevant judgments that might correct his assessment of his own classroom performance.

Despite the misuse of student learning indices and the bleak outlook ahead, there is unquestioned merit in continuing the research and the ongoing dialogue on these issues.

Chapter 7

Student Advising and Institutional Service

STUDENT ADVISING

College handbooks and catalogues are supposed to provide students with a simple, clear roadmap through the maze of undergraduate curriculum. With few notable exceptions, these handbooks and catalogues are at best dull reading and at worst impenetrable. To add to student woes, almost every curriculum has some unwritten requirements, for example, preferences for course sequence or elective courses, which become in effect visible but inflexible requirements for graduation.

In an effort to reduce student planning errors, colleges and universities have traditionally relied on faculty as student advisors in the planning. The faculty advisors often have to provide, without proper training, counseling to students on personal problems.

Generally, the faculty advisors are given responsibility for overseeing the number of credits taken per semester, the fulfillment of prerequisites, and the meeting of course and major requirements for graduation. Unfortunately, most students see their faculty advisors only long enough to get course approval during the frenzied registration process, with the result that impersonal, if not strained, relationships between students and advisors are often the norm.

As McKeachie (1978, p. 199) observes: "Although many catalogues will carry ambitious statements about faculty counseling conjuring up an image of the wise, genial, pipe-smoking academician in leisurely discussion with the eager, respectful student ... the stark reality of the relationship is often that of a meeting between a rebelliously impatient student and a harried and disgruntled faculty member."

Why harried and disgruntled? The task of academic advising has traditionally been a source of dissatisfaction for many faculty members. Burdened with course preparation, committee assignments, research commitments, many professors tend to look upon the student-advising hours as lost hours.

The professors' attitude is not lost on the students. In a survey of over 3400 undergraduates at 16 diverse institutions, Granger (1977) reports that more than 60 percent cite the need to improve the quality of faculty advising. Common complaints are that the faculty advisors lack familiarity with the curriculum, lack interest in the student as a person, and frequently are unavailable. A Fort Hays State University report (1978) comes up with similar findings. Asked for an appraisal of the advising process, the students cite these problem areas:

1. Too many students per advisor.
2. Some advisors lack knowledge about all the curriculum requirements.
3. Inadequate concern for the student's personal problems.
4. The meeting of advisor and student occurs only during the rush at registration.
5. The advisors are unavailable too often.

Student lamentations and faculty discomfort with the student-advising process are not confined to a few colleges and universities. The unhappy condition is practically endemic. In *The New York Times*, Fisk (1978, p. 9) is driven to the conclusion that "effective advisory systems are rare." Eble (1976, p. 74) agrees: "Formal advising is right now and everywhere in pretty much of a mess."

Ignored by Promotion Committees

Few faculty members seem to accept student advising as an integral part of their responsibilities. Thus, since sound advice is generally unavailable from faculty advisors on problems of course selection, career choice, and personal matters, the undergraduates turn to their peers for advice. The faculty advisor becomes a passive or invisible advisor.

It requires no shrewd guess at the underlying reason for this insupportable situation. Rarely are faculty members rewarded for their counseling. As Miller (1972, p. 41) puts it, professors who take "the time necessary for constructive, informed advising" are given "few, if any, 'brownie points.'" The result: benign neglect by most professors of their advisory role in favor of such practical considerations as the pursuit of teaching and research, areas in which the rewards of promotion in rank and tenure are invariably found. The day colleges and universities cease paying lip service to academic advising, faculty members will cease regarding it as a peripheral function. And students will receive professorial advice as part and parcel of the teacher-student relationship.

Upcoming Change

That day is perhaps dawning at last. So many additional curriculum options have opened in the past decade that the importance of student advising has been increasingly impressed on the faculty. Also, flexible programming for part-time and adult students is playing a part. And a tight job market is impelling more and more students to seek career guidance from faculty advisors. Economic uncertainty tends to turn students to the older, more experienced faculty member, rather than peers, for advice.

There is also the matter of student retention that is being placed on the front burner by administration and faculty. The expected shortage of college freshmen in the next decade is becoming a popular, if troublesome, topic behind closed academic doors. There are stark financial benefits to colleges and universities from persuading students not to drop out of school. The retention of students is viewed as vital to the financial health of the institution. The dreaded alternative is to close down the school.

Thus, orientation programs at many schools are being over-hauled. Faculty members are being sensitized to student problems serious enough to cause them to drop out. Crash programs to keep the classrooms full are beginning to operate on many campuses. The total impact of all this is beginning to reverse the traditional advisor-student relationship from largely a paper relationship to a real one.

At Drake University, for example, training programs to make faculty members more effective student advisors have helped push the retention rate in five years from 69 to 76 percent. Reed College integrated faculty participation in the freshman orientation program and enjoyed a retention rise from 72 to 82 percent from 1973 to 1977. At Central Washington University and Florida Junior College, programs to encourage faculty-student relationships outside the classroom had a salutary affect on freshman retention. At the University of Maryland a computer identifies academically-failing students who then receive an invitation to counseling by a faculty member. This program was initially developed for minority and other special students and has resulted in a 52 to 61 percent rise in their retention rate between 1974 and 1977.

Netusil and Hallenbeck (1975), in a study at Iowa State University, found that faculty advisors directly influenced a host of variables affecting student satisfaction. The researchers concluded that a good way to encourage student retention is to sensitize faculty advisors to student satisfactions.

EVALUATING FACULTY ADVISORS

In light of the rebirth of institutional interest in the faculty member as student advisor, the next step inevitably will be the need to evaluate the faculty member's advisory performance. Promotion and tenure committees, which historically have largely ignored this performance, will have to reverse gears. The advisory role will have to take its place among other factors given weight by the committees in faculty evaluation.

Sources of Information

It makes good sense to regard the students advised by the faculty member as a primary source of evaluative information. Supplementary information can be obtained from the department chairperson or advising coordinator, faculty colleagues, alumni, and even the advisor himself.

Some institutions find it useful to scrutinize the discrepancy between the advisor's self-evaluation and that of the advised students or the department chairperson. This approach is based on the assumption that discrepancies revealed to the advisor will produce such dissonance as to motivate the advisor to improve his performance. It also rests on the premise that the advisor wants to locate and erase advising weaknesses. To this end, at several institutions advising centers have been organized to help faculty members sharpen advisory skills. The number of such centers is expected to increase over the next years.

Choosing a Rating Form

The general procedure at many institutions commencing an evaluative program for faculty advisors is the naming of a committee to produce the rating form. The next step, if it is to put together an original rating form, can be lengthy and divisive. The more prudent step is to consider the rating forms, and the experience of other institutions. The universities of Maryland, Washington, Cornell, and the College of Saint-Francis (Illinois), for example, have developed rating forms and have considerable experience with them. (See samples, Forms 10 and 11.)

The Center for Faculty Evaluation and Development in Higher Education, at Kansas State University, has a developed and commercially available rating form. An institution subscribing to the service receives a detailed survey form (see Form 12) to be filled in by the advised students. The results are computer-scored and returned to each faculty advisor, revealing not only the students' evaluation but also the advisor's comparative standing at his institution.

Clearly, the borrowed rating form must fit well without pinching any of the advisory aims of the local institution. Adaptation may be required. Indeed, it is probably better to adapt than to adopt

111

another institution's rating scale to be certain that local needs are met.

But before adapting, it is essential to develop a clear, concise statement of objectives for the advisory program. In the very beginning, suggests Miller (1972, p. 42), "each institution will need to examine its commitment to the advising program; organization and procedure should follow from the basic philosophical and policy commitment. This commitment, if more than rhetoric, should be measurable."

Similar to student and peer evaluation, it is mandatory to encourage open discussion by faculty of the advisory program if confidence in, and support of, the program is to be gained. And at each stage of the program's development the decisions growing out of the discussions must be openly arrived at.

Selection of Included Items

Many rating forms ask questions about an advisor's accessibility, knowledge of relevant information, the extent of personal interest in his students. Overall, an appraisal of the advisor's competence should include judgments on:

(1) *Advisor knowledge.* Is the advisor well versed in the rules, programs, procedures and requirements? Is his knowledge current? How effectively does he transmit his knowledge to the students? Does he avoid registration and curricular errors?

(2) *Availability.* Is he available when students need advice throughout the semester? Does he post and maintain advising

Form 10.

STUDENT APPRAISAL OF ADVISING

Name of advisor _____

Dept. _____ Date _____

Please indicate your appraisal of your faculty advisor in regard to eight characteristics which students have indicated are important to them.

Read the description of each factor listed below. Draw a circle around the number that indicates your rating of your academic advisor.

112

Do this for each of the eight qualities, making each answer a separate judgment. Only in extremely rare cases will the circled number be the same for all qualities.

		Low				High
1.	Is genuinely interested in you and your problems.	1	2	3	4	5
2.	Keeps regular office hours and is readily available for advising.	1	2	3	4	5
3.	Is friendly and approachable.	1	2	3	4	5
4.	Provides alternatives but encourages you to assume responsibility for decisions.	1	2	3	4	5
5.	Understands your point of view.	1	2	3	4	5
6.	Has both current and thorough knowledge of courses and requirements.	1	2	3	4	5
7.	Maintains accurate files on your progress.	1	2	3	4	5
8.	Composite rating.	1	2	3	4	5

You are invited to comment further on the effectiveness of your academic advisor especially in areas not covered by the questions.

_____

_____

_____

_____

_____

_____

_____

_____

hours? Does he encourage students to return for follow-up help if required?

(3) *Interest in students.* Is he genuinely interested in students, their performance and problems? Is he friendly toward them? Does he treat them as individuals? Does he seek out students to invite discussion on matters of joint concern? Does he know students by their first name and is he aware of their individual interests, hobbies, etc.?

Form 11.

STUDENT APPRAISAL OF ADVISING

Name of advisor _____

Dept._____Date _____

The following items reflect basic components of academic advising.

Please rate your faculty advisor by drawing a circle around the number that most closely expresses your view.

		Low				High
1.	Maintains office hours and is readily available for academic advising.	1	2	3	4	5
2.	Is friendly and warm toward you.	1	2	3	4	5
3.	Keeps up-to-date in curricular requirements and course offerings.	1	2	3	4	5
4.	Helps you understand course requirements and registration procedures.	1	2	3	4	5
5.	Offers alternatives in making decisions but final judgment is left to you.	1	2	3	4	5
6.	Offers helpful counsel in solving academic problems.	1	2	3	4	5
7.	Expresses interest in your non-academic problems.	1	2	3	4	5
8.	Has personal interest in assisting you through advising.	1	2	3	4	5
9.	Seeks to plan programs consistent with your stated career objectives.	1	2	3	4	5
10.	Considering everything, how would you rate this faculty advisor?	1	2	3	4	5

11. What did your faculty advisor do that you found particularly helpful? Please specify.

12. What could your faculty advisor have done to be more helpful? Please specify.

(4) *Scope of advising.* How wide-ranging is his discussion? Does it encompass the student's academic program and go on to discuss life, education, career goals? Is he interested in helping the student resolve non-academic problems?

(5) *Referral.* Is he able to refer students to additional sources of information? Does he effectively use these sources?

(6) *Method of advising.* Does he present information clearly? Is the advisory time used efficiently? Does he adapt methods to meet new situations? Is his choice of language appropriate and effective? Is his effectiveness weakened by distracting mannerisms?

(7) *Earnest concern for advising.* Does he show signs of enjoying advising? Is he interested in improving advising by self-analysis of performance and/or by trying innovative approaches? Does he seek out colleagues to discuss advising improvement?

(8) *Overall.* What changes are needed to improve the advising performance? Which aspects of the advising were particularly effective, ineffective? How does this advisor compare with others in the department? In the institution?

Crockett (1977) suggests that a useful appraisal instrument should include items such as length and frequency of student contact, topics discussed, accessibility, number of referrals, student satisfaction, number of registration errors, retention rate of students, and knowledge of the institution.

If the ratings of advisors are employed to improve performance, it is helpful to include several open-end questions to elicit replies in the respondent's own words: "List the three traits you liked most about this advisor." "What is the most unsatisfactory characteristic of this advisor?"

But, if the ratings are to be employed in personnel decisions, a standardized 1-5 response scale is probably best since it simplifies tallying and interpreting the responses on the rating form.

Administering the Rating Form

To heighten the validity and utility of the responses on the rating form, certain common pitfalls need to be avoided. These include: (a) irregular administering of the rating form, (b) improper instruction leading to biased results, (c) lack of performance

Form 12.
ADVISING SURVEY FORM

Your Advisor's Name: _____

Your College/University: _____

Your Academic Major: _____ Your Age: _____

Your thoughtful answers to these questions will provide helpful information to your advisor. Please answer each question by writing the appropriate number in the space provided.

_____ 1. How many times have you met (for 10 minutes or more) with your current advisor?

   1 = I have *not* met with my advisor
   2 = One
   3 = Two or Three
   4 = Four or Five
   5 = Six or more

_____ 2. How long have you had your current advisor?

   1 = 1–6 Months
   2 = 7–12 Months
   3 = 13–18 Months
   4 = 19–24 Months
   5 = Over 2 Years

_____ 3. I am:

   1 = Female
   2 = Male

_____ 4. My advisor is:

   1 = Female
   2 = Male

_____ 5. What is your classification?

   1 = First year
   2 = Second year
   3 = Third year
   4 = Fourth year
   5 = Other

How descriptive of your meetings with your advisor is each of the following? Rate questions 6–33 using the following key:

Not at all descriptive (least accurate)				Very descriptive (most accurate)
1	2	3	4	5

My Advisor:
_____ 6. Asked me questions about my college experience.
_____ 7. Used knowledge of his/her own field of specialization in advising.
_____ 8. Kept well informed about my progress by checking with me.

116

———— 9. Asked for clarification as a means for understanding what I was saying.
————10. Summarized my comments.
————11. Looked directly at me while we were talking.
————12. Used knowledge of courses and course-content to aid me.
————13. Checked to see if I understood what he/she was saying.
————14. Did *not* encourage me to talk about my knowledge and experience.
————15. Used knowledge of career opportunities in advising.
————16. Clearly described his/her responsibilities as advisor.
————17. Seemed relaxed while talking with me.
————18. Put limits on the types of topics I could bring up.
————19. Asked me to specify a goal or goals.
————20. Explored with me the obstacles I need to overcome to reach my goal(s).
————21. Asked me to list the options or choices I had.
————22. Suggested that I set a time-table for reaching my gaols.
————23. Used knowledge of rules/regulations of the college in advising.
————24. Challenged me to higher academic performance.
————25. Refused to endorse a course of action I had planned.
————26. Established procedures which made it easy to get in touch with her/him.
————27. Was willing to discuss my feelings and emotions.
————28. Used knowledge of postgraduate opportunities in advising.
————29. Gave me *incorrect* information about academic regulations.
————30. Avoided discussing my personal problems.
————31. Seemed in a hurry to end our meetings.
————32. When advising on a specific concern, discussed its impact on my total academic program.
————33. Suggested other people (or offices) from whom I could seek help.

Rate your advisor's helpfulness in each of the following areas. For those items which are *not* applicable to your relationship with your advisor, write "0" in the space provided; otherwise use the following key:

Definitely *not* helpful . Very helpful

. 1	2	3	4	5

————34. Deciding upon a course schedule.
————35. Picking courses appropriate to my abilities and interests.
————36. Exploring majors of interest to me.
————37. Developing my interest in an academic discipline.
————38. Advising me about opportunities for graduate study and programs.
————39. Exploring vocational possibilities and interests with me.
————40. Being someone on campus I can depend on.
————41. Being someone I can discuss personal concerns with.
————42. Achieving a more realistic understanding of my goals.
————43. Encouraging my personal and intellectual growth (independent of course and career selection).
————44. Cutting through institutional red-tape.

Answer questions 45–52 considering the *results* of your relationship with your faculty advisor using the following key:

Strongly *Disagree* Strongly Agree

1	2	3	4	5

_____45. I am more confident in pursuing my academic program.
_____46. I feel better able to make a career choice.
_____47. I am better able to handle my personal problems.
_____48. My advisor has significantly influenced my choice of academic major.
_____49. If it weren't for my advisor, I would have dropped out of school or transferred to another institution.
_____50. I understand how to achieve my goals within this institution. (i.e., I understand the graduation requirements, how to proceed on academic and other matters, etc.)
_____51. I will be prepared to seek a job or pursue further study.
_____52. Overall, I consider my advisor to be a good advisor.

Source: Center for Faculty Evaluation and Development in Higher Education and Howard C. Kramer and Robert E. Gardner (1978). Reproduced by permission of the authors.

standards making meaningful interpretation virtually impossible.

A suggested first step is a "dry run" on a representative sample of students. The students and advisors will probably profit from the experience. In the trial run the students and advisors have an opportunity to identify and correct ambiguities, biases and poor phrasing.

The rating form can be administered two weeks before the term ends, prior to registration for the next semester. It can be administered once or twice each year as local conditions warrant. In general, department chairpersons and/or advising coordinators should complete the form once yearly for non-tenured faculty and every second year for tenured faculty.

The exact administrative procedure will vary of course from institution to institution. But regardless of the procedure adopted, the very heart of the rating form depends entirely on the confidence and trust the respondents place in it. Those answering the questions must fully understand the purposes for which their responses will be used. Any loss of confidence or trust will translate immediately to diminished student motivation and advisor resentment.

Using the Information

The growing acceptance of the principle of evaluating advisory performance has placed a premium on the appropriate use of the evaluation. How does a faculty advisor know if his rating is good, average, poor? How does it compare with peer ratings? The questions are easily answered if the institution has developed an interpretation manual showing the norms for the institution. The closer the normative comparison (for example, academic advisor to biology majors), the more meaningful the data comparison.

If ratings on advisory performance are for personnel decisions, an overall rating ("How do you rate this faculty advisor compared to others in the department?") is advisable.

Brock (1978), in a study of 700 students advised by 78 faculty members, found that ratings by 10 students provide reliable information (the average corrected correlation for split halves was .69). He also discovered that neither the student expectations about the advisory process nor the sex and year of the student had any apparent affect on the student's rating of the advisory performance.

Nevertheless, it is prudent to supplement student ratings with departmental chairperson, advising coordinator, and even faculty colleague and alumni appraisals. A wide variation in any of their ratings should be cause for searching inquiry.

If ratings on advisory performance are for improvement of that performance, specific practices should be appraised. To this end, many colleges and universities appoint a coordinator of advisors. As the advisor of advisors, he helps them confront, understand and act on practices to improve performance. He probes motivation, sorts out their practices, sharpens skills, adds knowledge. He is responsible for an umbrella program of advisory improvement.

The department chairperson can play an important role in the advisory program. He can alert advisors to curricular changes and can underscore the importance of quality advising as a vehicle for student retention in the department and the institution. By his own counseling of faculty advisors he is acting as a model.

Innovative and Successful Advising Programs
With an eye on improving the quality of faculty advising and thereby decreasing student attrition, some institutions have torn down and reconstructed their advising programs. Texas Christian University, for example, now offers a centralized advisory program for freshmen and undeclared majors. Because such students traditionally have the highest drop-out rate, the TCU program ventures far beyond the scheduling of courses. Carefully selected advisors work closely with a maximum of 20 students to explore careers and program options. In addition to vocational and academic counseling, personal-problem counseling is integral to the advisor's responsibilities. The objective is to help the freshmen and undeclared majors to overcome any stumbling block to an academic degree.

The University of California, in an innovative approach, has developed an undergraduate course which offers credit and training to students interested in becoming peer counselors. The program brings experienced professionals as class teachers, and early reports on the effectiveness of the approach are very encouraging.

The College of Business, at Arizona State University, operates a program in which the responsibility for student advising is divided between a central advisement center and faculty advisors. The center handles the students through the sophomore year and then turns them over to faculty advisors for the junior and senior years. The program's rationale is that during their first two years students are primarily concerned with fulfilling general curricular requirements (social and behavioral science, mathematics, the humanities). They select these courses from the several colleges within Arizona State University. Graduate students, who are trained in curricular requirements, work closely with the freshmen and sophomores out of the advisement center. The special expertise of the faculty advisors is brought to play during the more pressing junior and senior years.

A few institutions offer faculty members the quid pro quo of released time or lighter teaching loads in return for becoming faculty advisors. This offer was first made by Bradley University almost 30 years ago. It may soon be the vogue as institutions attempt to turn around the alarming student drop-out rate.

Institutional Commitment

If any influence can be singled out as the most important to an effective faculty advisory program it is the commitment of the institution to the program. Effective advisory programs are costly in human, fiscal and physical terms. No substitute has yet been found for sturdy and open institutional support.

Grites and Metz (1977, p. 6) offer these suggestions as overt institutional demonstrations of support:

"1. Make academic advising a formal part of the evaluation process for faculty members.

2. Establish explicit criteria for selecting and appointing academic advisors.

3. Develop a clear statement of advisor function and role.

4. Academic advisors (should be) appointed by Dean, Provost or similar administrative person.

5. Select a campus-wide, 'Blue-Ribbon' group to evaluate the state of advising. Members to be appointed by the Chancellor, President, or Provost."

Communicating the Institutional Commitment

Obviously, it is not enough for the institution simply to have a support policy; it must be effectively communicated to faculty and students. The administration must hammer out the policy to fit its clearly defined objectives. The students' advisory needs require identification, and who and how to meet the needs requires thoughtful decision. Responsibility and authority require clean definition.

To insure deep and widespread understanding of the objectives and methods of the program, newsletters can serve as a regular channel of information. Administrators can meet periodically with faculty advisors to transmit curricular changes and other pieces of useful information. A few institutions have created an "Advisor of the Year" award which is bestowed with campus eclat to signify administrative program support.

Choosing Faculty Advisors

Although a few institutions have successfully assigned all faculty members as advisors, most institutions consider it more advisable to select only the faculty members meeting fixed criteria. Most crucial in the selective process is genuine interest in working with students as advisor. Another criterion is the ability to deal with students as individuals and human beings. Empathy, warmth, intuition and flexibility are mandatory characteristics. The patience to listen, the willingness to gather considerable data required by students are also needed characteristics. And the faculty member selected as advisor must be willing to give as much time as necessary to counsel students on courses, careers, personal problems.

Doubtless, every institution has some faculty members embodying all these characteristics, and have the makings of effective advisors. Chances are, they are also outstanding teachers in the classroom.

Advisee Load

How many students can one advisor manage properly? The number depends on the advisor's competence, the discipline, the students' class level, the personal preference of advisor and students, the policies of the institution. It also depends on the advisor's teaching load, research and publication commitments, and committee assignments. Adjustments should be made to achieve maximum advisory load consistent with other faculty obligations.

Which students are likely to need special attention? Astin (1975), in a nationwide study, found them to be students who have poor high school records, low grades, poor study habits, been raised by low-income, poorly educated Protestant parents, are married females, are habitual smokers. There were other factors also likely to be found in students in need of special counseling.

Training

Even if naturally endowed with all the desired characteristics, most faculty members must be trained to handle the role of advisor competently. The advisory skills can be taught and learned with no more travail than other professional skills. The advisor learns by receiving instruction, by study, by practicing.

Many institutions have organized formal training programs for advisors. At James Madison University, for example, workshops are held on academic areas not adequately covered in the catalogue. These areas include program requirements, grades and retention, attendance, appeal or waiver procedures, course substitution, testing programs.

A sequence of six training modules, described by Grites and Metz (1977), has been developed for faculty advisors at Stockton State College.

1. *Basic information skills.* Complete, accurate knowledge of academic rules, policies, procedures, regarding major course requirements, registration procedures, retention policies.

2. *Career development and decision-making skills.* Compatability of a student's objectives with his limitations, motivations, collateral interests. Investigation of optional careers, sharpening decision-making skills.

3. *Communication skills.* The development of credibility and confidence in an advisor, identification of non-verbal communication, and facilitating communication by action statements and appropriate referrals.

4. *Co-curricular activities.* The involvement of students in experimental learning programs, student government, residence hall and campus activities to enhance their curricular goals.

5. *Environmental perspective.* The development in the advisor of an appreciative understanding of minority students, returning women, gifted students, handicapped, older students, and the main body of standard students.

6. *Developmental perspective.* The integration and synthesis of the previous five modules.

At the University of Maryland, the Center for Undergraduate Advising conducts periodic workshops which keep faculty informed of changes in requirements, policies, procedures at the university, division and department levels. At Oakton Community College, the faculty is invited to training programs designed to explain the advisory process and thus develop advisory skills.

In addition to in-house training, some institutions enroll their advisors in seminars on the topic conducted by organizations such as The American College Testing Program.

Advising Handbook

Faculty members cannot be expected to answer all student questions from memory, and an invaluable aid is a comprehensive, well-indexed handbook. Such handbook is a quick and accurate resource guide. For optimum use, it should be current. It should contain detailed information on academic policies, grading, testing, degree requirements, registration, special programs, academic support or remedial services, referrals and waivers. For added use, it should contain the institution's regulations on automobiles, dormitory living, and other non-academic topics. The comprehensive handbook will also contain advisory tips and a clear statement on the advisor's responsibility and authority.

Conclusion

Far too many colleges and universities are operating with inadequate advisory programs. Sometimes the inadequacy stems from adopting rather than adapting another institution's program. What works well in one institution may work badly in another. Close attention must be paid to fit the program to the institution.

Beyond the program is the problem of the ability and interest of the faculty advisor to perform effectively. Success as an advisor is link-chained to ready access by students to the advisor, the possession of specific and accurate information and communicative skills, and the nurturing of a caring and personal advisor-student relationship. Since these requirements are measurable, the competency of advisors needs periodic evaluation. This evaluation is part of the overall evaluation of the whole teacher.

INSTITUTIONAL SERVICE

It is recognized and unquestioned that some kind of institutional service is part of the responsibility of each faculty member. The kind of service varies with each institution.

One institution construes service as the teacher's relationship, attitude, behavior within the department or the institution. Another sees it in the teacher's willingness to shoulder a heavy workload of less desirable courses. Still another recognizes it in the discharge of extra administrative duties.

The leading indices of institutional service, however, are academic advising and participation on department or institution-wide committees (see Chapter 2).

In general, faculty members are occupied in varying degree with service activities and most allot a fair amount of valuable time to the function. Inevitably, a few faculty members seem to give service a top priority. Soon they occupy influential positions in internal governance, particularly in large universities, and at times at the cost of declining quality in their teaching, research and publication.

It is a popular assumption that every faculty member is an expert in his specialty, and it seems almost as popular to believe that he can

Form 13.
APPRAISAL OF FACULTY SERVICE

Faculty member _____

Dept._____Date _____

Appraiser_____Title _____

The following elements reflect basic components of faculty service and relations.

Please rate the faculty member named above by drawing a circle around the number that most closely expresses your view.

		Low				High	Don't Know
1.	Attends committee and faculty meetings regularly.	1	2	3	4	5	X
2.	Does an appropriate share of institutional service assignments.	1	2	3	4	5	X
3.	Accepts service assignments willingly.	1	2	3	4	5	X
4.	Makes a positive contribution to assigned committees.	1	2	3	4	5	X
5.	Serves effectively as a committee chairperson.	1	2	3	4	5	X
6.	Maintains a professional and cooperative attitude in dealing with colleagues.	1	2	3	4	5	X
7.	Actively supports departmental and institutional goals.	1	2	3	4	5	X
8.	Is prompt and accurate with reports, grades, etc.	1	2	3	4	5	X
9.	Is genuinely interested in assisting colleagues.	1	2	3	4	5	X
10.	Composite rating.	1	2	3	4	5	X

Nature of faculty assignments and services:

_____

_____

You are invited to comment further on the effectiveness of this faculty member especially in areas not covered by the questions.

_____

_____

_____

_____

_____

function effectively on any and all committees. As a result of this assumption faculty members can find themselves assigned to such committees as institutional governance, student activities, parking facilities and regulations, and campus security. Sometimes it seems that faculty members spend endless hours in endless meetings.

It is apparently no less an article of faith to believe that the sheer length of a teacher's committee list equates to his dedication to the institution. Even when personnel decisions are made, few institutions take the trouble to assess the quality of the service. The unfortunate result is that the appraisal of the teacher's performance is at times neither systematic nor reliable.

Evaluating Service

As with systematic evaluation of every aspect of faculty performance, standardized rating forms are essential (see Form 13 for a sample rating form to appraise service).

Quality of institutional service can be judged as demonstrated by several colleges and universities which have developed the necessary yardsticks. These depend not only on the institution's size and organization structure but also on the institution's goals and the teachers' activities on their behalf. Following are some useful criteria and guiding questions:

1. *Acceptance of service assignments*. Does the faculty member accept assignments willingly? Does he occasionally volunteer? Is he willing to assume a variety of assignments?

2. *Committee work*. Does he attend committee meetings regularly? Does he come to the meetings prepared? Carry out committee assignments? Are his contributions disruptive of the

committee? How do his fellow members perceive his committee performance?

3. *Committee chairperson.* Is he an effective chairperson? Does he make efficient use of each member's knowledge and skills by assigning appropriate tasks to each? Does he keep the committee's work on schedule? Does he encourage passive members and curb impulsive members, skillfully? Does he handle dissent maturely? Does he husband the committee's time to be sure it is well spent?

4. *Faculty relations.* Is the faculty member always civil toward his colleagues? Toward others? Does he show respect for differing opinions? Is he cooperative? Does he offer department peers help with their problems? How much of an asset to his department is he?

5. *Cooperative attitude.* Does he appear interested and pleased to carry out assignments? Act in the best interests of the department? Of the institution? Is he positive and forward-looking? Responsive to others' needs?

6. *Overall.* How do you rate his institutional service contribution against others in the department? In the institution? What suggestions do you make to strengthen his performance?

The department chairperson and faculty colleagues are in an advantageous position for insights on performance. Their personal observations are considerably more worthwhile than hearsay or cloakroom gossip. The teacher's self-evaluation is also useful in itself and as a foil.

Faculty members bring to their service assignments varying degrees of interest and skills. As a result, some are more effective than others. How effective is not difficult to determine. And that determination should be part of the teacher's overall performance. It is the responsibility of the institution to provide workshops or other training seminars for teachers who are desirous of improving their performance. That desire should be shared by the institution.

Chapter 8

Research and Publication

How important is research and publication in the evaluation of faculty performance? How important compared to classroom teaching? Can a teacher do a good job in the classroom without also engaging in original research in his field? These questions have generated hot arguments but no final answers over the years.

These questions have also generated some purple prose. Levesque (1977, p. 32) points an accusatory finger at some institutions where the word publish "evokes images of tumbrells rolling through the streets of Revolutionary Paris.... Failure to publish may invite professional extinction or exile to Northern Manitoba."

Publish or perish is "the most damnably successful alliteration in higher education," charges Drake (1976, p. 1), and he further charges that "scarcely a cow college in the country has not, at one time or another, had this phrase raised as a rallying cry, and with it spectres of demonic deans and superannuated professors, twisted by hate, wedded to the notion of mediocrity in higher education, determined to stamp out any spark of light in the ashes of the classroom."

There are more than 2,000 colleges and universities in the U.S. and as would be expected there is wide latitude in their assessment of both quantity and quality of research and publication. In general, the relative weight given research and publication, on the one hand, and classroom teaching, on the other, depends on the institution's purposes, traditions, prestige, resources, faculty and students.

The larger, older colleges and universities seem to favor as an institutional policy research and publication over teaching. This seems particularly true in institutions with strong graduate programs. The moderate-size and small institutions seem to stand four-square behind classroom teaching. This can be inferred from their catalogues' insistent embracing of "quality teaching." Nevertheless, the salary, promotion and tenure of faculty in these smaller institutions are contingent to some degree on faculty engagement with research and publication.

127

Caplow and McGee (1958) conclude that professors may be paid to teach but they are evaluated in terms of their research contributions. This view is shared by those faculty members, and their numbers are legion, who have experienced the sting of punishment from personnel committees dominated by professors upholding the importance of scholarship.

What is the origin of research in academic life? It developed first in the universities of nineteenth century Prussia. It jumped the Atlantic and took firm root in the U.S. in the years immediately preceding the First World War. Today it is in full bloom. Defined in the *London Times Higher Education Supplement* as the "institutionalization of scholarship," research is the sine qua non of excellence in many colleges and universities of world renown. However, the celebration of research in academe is not without its detractors. A few give utterance to their objections but most silently accommodate to the domineering role of research in higher education.

The Value of Research.

In general, five major reasons are offered to support the importance of research.

First, aspiring scholars can find no better way to advance their professionalism, and the general knowledge in their field, than in original research. And their promotion and tenure rest on their research capabilities.

Second, teaching morale in higher education is intimately associated with research as is the prestige and interest generated by new ideas that act as inducements for students to seek careers in the field.

Third, research in itself is a honing of the teacher's intellectual powers and thus indirectly tends to sharpen and improve classroom performance. A researcher brings an extra dimension of keen wit to the classroom.

Fourth, societal recognition of the teacher arrives sooner with research and publication, particularly when newsworthy, than of the teacher who confines his brilliance to the classroom. The latter teacher has difficulty demonstrating his classroom brilliance in front of questioning personnel committees. Dean Henry Rosovsky (1977, p. 23), of Harvard University, warns his teachers not to dedicate themselves to improved classroom performance at the expense of research. To do so, would throw away "the substantial evidence of research" which would "establish their reputation in the field outside of Harvard...."

Fifth, and the most widely expressed justification of research, is that it pushes back the frontiers of knowledge as a problem-solver and thus enlarges mankind's intellectual warehouse. The scholar is in demand for his inquiring mind and restless pursuit of elusive truth.

Relating Research and Publication.

Not all academic research is conducted by faculty members. Some of it is carried out in the biosciences, physics and engineering by doctoral research staff members who are neither faculty members nor have formal ties with any university department. They are in pursuit of pure research careers. In 1977, according to McGrath (1979), this group of researchers totaled about 4,200 and represented about 3 percent of all scientists and engineers with doctorates employed in academe. Although small, this select group is fast growing. Between 1975 and 1977 it increased by 20 percent, about 2½ times the faculty growth rate. It is speculated that higher education institutions are hiring non-faculty researchers as a method of coping with declining student enrollment, financial distress and skimpy research budgets.

Research and publication are not as closely hitched as the song-honored horse and buggy. Some research is aimed at utilitarian problems and never reaches print. Some publications are anything but research oriented. But most research is conducted with ultimate publication in mind and a rundown of a professor's published work is the generally accepted measure of his quantity and quality of research contributions.

Professors' Publication Output.

It is one of the more widely accepted assumptions that professors as a group are scholars of a high order who dig scientifically and write up their discoveries in the intellectual and scientific journals. A notable group of professors follow this behavior. And a prodigious volume of words are printed in the journals. But this torrent gushes from relatively few typewriters.

Bourgeois (1967) found that 90 percent of the published research was produced by 10 percent of the faculty at the University of Southwestern Louisiana. Heywood (1967) reported that only 11 percent of the faculty in Colleges of Advanced Technology, in England, saw their research reach print.

In the Ladd-Lipset survey (1977) of 4,400 faculty members at 161 colleges and universities in the U.S., 58 percent of the professors had not published a solitary book or monograph. About one-third had never published a scholarly article in the social sciences, humanities, business, agriculture, physical sciences or education. A handful of professors busily turned out all the published research.

Heiss (1968) advances the belief that 85 to 90 percent of higher education teaching is by professors who have removed themselves from research and publication. Ladd-Lipset (1975) suggest that most professors perceive themselves as teachers and professionals and not scholars and intellectuals. If so, they accept as fact that they do not possess seminal minds and content themselves with picking over the work of more energetic and original thinkers.

In fact, how much do professors value research?

Despite the popular impression that they value research above all other professional activities, several recent studies suggest that this is erroneous. A Ladd-Lipset nationwide survey (1975) came up with 25 percent of fulltime faculty acknowledging heavy interest in research, and 4 percent very heavy. Seventy-five percent gave higher interest priority to teaching with 37 percent giving it highest priority.

Similar findings are reported by Goldstein and Anderson (1977). They asked the University of Illinois faculty members to assume they could allocate their personal time. Research was clearly in second place behind teaching for almost two-thirds of the faculty.

Crow (1979) reports a survey at the University of Texas, at Arlington, which inquired into faculty interest in teaching and research. Twenty-five percent of the faculty preferred research and 5 percent stated strong preference.

The consistent conclusion in each of these studies is that higher education teachers in the U.S. overwhelmingly prefer teaching over research. Nevertheless, in the teeth of this nationwide preference, Miller (1974, p. 18) affirms that "every college teacher needs to be an occasional, if modest, producer of research or creative work in his field; or at least a careful and systematic student of the research and creativity of others...." Who can quarrel with that? Anything less makes it dubious for a teacher to keep abreast of his discipline. And how good a teacher will he be then?

Literature on the Correlation of Research and Teaching

Few would deny that the successful teacher must maintain currency in his field's knowledge and skills. But the critical question is, how does research correlate with teaching? Is the proficient and prolific researcher also the better teacher?

The literature is alive with position papers and studies on these questions. Jencks and Riesman (1969, pp. 532-3) argue for a positive relationship between research and teaching and insist that "when a teacher stops doing (research), he begins to repeat himself and eventually loses touch with both the young and the world around him."

Drake (1976, p. 4) is convinced that no matter how adequate the teaching performance of the professor, he could do even better by applying in the classroom the thoughtfulness and creativity he

130

exercised in his research. "Without research, the (teaching) scholar becomes stale and repetitive; his critical facilities wither; self-evident truths become dogma."

Levesque (1977, p. 32) argues that a good teacher must publish. He will be "an even more effective teacher if he pursues an untiring search for knowledge and (does not) . . . limit his audience (to the students)."

On the other hand, scoffers of the research-teaching relationship are also numerous and equally vocal. Bligh (1975, p. 217) attacks the belief, cherished mostly by teachers who do research, that good researchers necessarily make good teachers. He sees teaching and research as independent abilities and finds "no evidence" to the contrary.

Eble (1976, p. 18-19) also argues that research and teaching are not necessarily complementary. He segments the relationship in a "common sense" position. "Some good researchers are good teachers; some good researchers are poor teachers." And vice versa. Eble polishes off the problem by concluding that "the majority of both researchers and teachers are mediocre. . . ."

McIntyre (1977, p. 1) is persuaded that the research-teaching relationship is "erroneous."

There were many early studies of the relationship whose conclusions were so contradictory that they immolated each other. In 1950 Riley, Ryan and Lifschitz reported that professors who published received higher student ratings than professors who did not. McGrath (1962) agreed. He reported that two-thirds of the outstanding teachers in 15 liberal arts colleges had recently published at least one article. Bresler (1968) found that Tufts University students gave their highest ratings to teachers who were published researchers.

Positive but low correlations (about .25) between student ratings of teachers and the teachers' annual output of publications, were reported by Stallings and Singhal (1969). A "spill-over effect" in which research discoveries carried over into the classroom and thus enhanced the learning environment, was found by Linsky and Strauss (1975).

On the contrary, other investigators have reported studies which turned up no research-teaching relationship, or at best only a mildly positive one.

Voeks (1962) found no relationship at the University of Washington. Neither Hoyt (1970) at Kansas State University nor Hayes (1971) at Carnegie-Mellon University found a significant relationship between faculty research and the student ratings of the faculty. Mention must be made, however, of Hayes' finding of a significant positive relationship of the chairmen's evaluations of the faculties' research and teaching. Hayes explained this finding as perhaps a "halo effect."

McDaniel and Feldhusen (1970), in a sample of 76 professors and 4,484 students at Purdue University, turned up significant negative correlations (-.22 to -.30) between first authorship of books and student ratings of teachers. They also reported negative correlations (to -.23) for first authorship of articles. And no significant research-teaching relationship when measured against grants received by faculty.

In a review of the literature, Follman, Lantz and Anderson (1973) conclude that the research-teaching correlation is extremely low.

Dent and Lewis (1976) consider the number of citations in the Social Sciences Citation Index as a yardstick of prolific research. A comparison with student evaluations for 90 faculty members was then made. Dent and Lewis included all ranks and four academic departments in the study. They found no significant correlations between teaching effectiveness and 1) academic rank, 2) total number of publications, 3) number of citations by colleagues in the same or other disciplines, 4) earliest or most recent citations, 5) student evaluations. The researchers conclude that institutions hiring teachers solely on the merit of research are hiring teachers indistinguishable in classroom competency from their non-published colleagues.

Rossman (1976), in a study of 93 teachers at Macalester College, applies a point rating scale to the books and articles published by the teachers as a measure of their productivity. A questionnaire filled out by more than 200 students and 93 teachers identified the outstanding teachers. Product-moment and point biserial correlation coefficients were used to examine the possible relationship between publication and teaching. Statistical analysis showed no correlation.

Research—Often Only Indirectly Related to Teaching

Demonstrably, research conducted by teachers is often indirectly, if at all, related to classroom teaching. Few professors devote class time to a discussion of their own research areas. In fact, a professor's research may be at odds with his teaching responsibilities in several ways:

First, the specialized character of most research does not lend itself to the general subject matter of most undergraduate courses.

Second, the man-hours devoted to research may be hours borrowed from teaching preparation, or at least might be devoted to some aspect of teaching.

Third, the deep personal satisfactions associated with research and publication, which will be read by hundreds or thousands of

132

one's peers, are of a different order from the satisfactions associated with the mind expansion of a class of nineteen- or twenty-year olds.

Fourth, since the current reward system at most colleges and universities favors research and publication, professors dedicating their energies wholeheartedly to classroom teaching may find their faculty positions in jeopardy.

Fifth, researchers set their own hours and pace whereas teachers are restricted to hourly classes scheduled in advance by administrators.

Sixth, the methodology of research is at opposite poles from the methodology of teaching. Each requires separate and distinct skills and motivation. Salter (1977) sees the two as incompatible. Some administrators have even resigned their posts contending that the institution concentrates on research at the expense of teaching (for example, Robert Marshall, former dean, College of Arts and Sciences, University of Pittsburgh).

Seventh, especially in larger institutions with a publish-or-perish Damocles sword suspended overhead, professors who want to be effective teachers are tugged in opposite directions. They must consign sizeable blocs of time simultaneously to research and to teaching. Mannon and Traicoff (1976), in an attempt to straddle the opposing demands, suggest the exploration and uncovering of some research areas which are more closely related to the teaching process.

Although the teachers in colleges and universities are diverse in a host of characteristics, nevertheless they are of two reasonably distinct and somewhat opposing types. One type, comments Eble (1976, p. 19) "likes to work alone, responds poorly to outside distractions and pressures, is more at ease with the stuff of ideas, facts and materials of a discipline than with students and learning." The other type "seeks out company, can handle pressures and distractions, and prefers interacting with students to manipulate materials or ideas." Eble believes that the scholar-teacher combining both types is "recognizable" and "anomalous."

Some teachers are not particularly successful because they are joyless in instructing students. Others are unsuccessful but learn to accommodate to teaching as an unpleasant but necessary means to pursue scholarly research. The good teacher who is also a good researcher remains the Holy Grail for many institutions.

ASSESSING RESEARCH AND PUBLICATION

Without doubt, most colleges and universities rely on research and publication as the litmus test in making faculty promotion and tenure decisions. But the test often appears to be makeshift and subjective. Too often, the judgments are neither the result of formal measuring instruments nor expressed in quantitative terms. As one professor sums up today's practice at his institution: "It's very simple. We look at all the publications. Then the committee gets together and we have a gut reaction."

The actual practice of assessing research and publication varies of course from institution to institution. But the core problems in the assessment are the same for all institutions.

1. The institution must make known its preference, or how it weighs, basic versus applied research, as guidance for its professors. Otherwise, professors may follow their own penchant for research and the assessment committee will be at a loss for an institutional yardstick.

2. Not infrequently, research spans several years and imposes the additional burden of trying to judge the quality of the research before it is finished. Promotion and tenure decisions may hang on such judgment.

3. When several faculty members coauthor an article the contribution of each author must be weighed. This is an exceedingly difficult task.

4. While many articles are based on research, others rest on theoretical considerations. How are the latter to be valued? The brain-power demanded for each type of article may be equal. As springboards for further research, they may be equal. How are they to be weighted by the institution?

Many institutions rely on a nose-count of a professor's published articles in evaluating the professor's performance, a hazardous procedure at best. Some professors can write 10 articles while others rewrite the same article 10 times. Some professors can churn out lightweight articles (not worth the sacrifice of a tree) while others spend years on a seminal monograph.

Wolf (1978, p. 16) warns against judging a teacher's productivity exclusively on numbers. "Of what value is productivity measured in terms of (the) ... number of articles? What does this tell colleagues, potential students, administrators or legislators? That Department X has produced more trivia than Department Y? That the faculty at X can slice the baloney into smaller (and therefore more numerous) articles than Department Y?"

Implicit in this approach is the assumption that one suit will fit men of all sizes, a piece of simplistic nonsense. Yet there are arguments that any article printed in a refereed journal is of good quality. Perhaps. This approach discounts the backgrounds and personal preferences of the referees. Some reject submitted articles not because of dubious scholarship but because the philosophic viewpoints are not consonant with the referees. Some favor short articles, others long ones. Some reject articles in one discipline that would be accepted, because of a different set of standards, in another discipline.

Even counting only refereed journals as bona fide publications is an inadequate practice since many excellent periodicals are not refereed. The past decade has witnessed a proliferation of academic and professional journals. The reasons? One, is the need to communicate rapidly in a fast-changing environment. Another, is to offer more outlets for professors to meet the publish-or-perish syndrome. The *Directory of Publishing Opportunities*, in its most recent edition (1975), lists more than 2,600 specialized and professional journals which accept manuscripts in English. Many journals though of high quality are not refereed. Simple justice requires that the quality of both the article and journal be judged rather than the journal's refereed or non-refereed status.

Developing a System to Assess Research and Publication

Professors may differ widely and vociferously on the place of research and publication in their overall evaluation. But most colleges and universities accord an honored place to research and publication in the evaluation of faculty. How much honor depends on the institution.

At some institutions, faculty members who elect to dedicate most of their waking time to a major research program are excused by the department chairman or dean from many faculty responsibilities. At other institutions, research and publication are accepted but not encouraged, and professors are expected to go about their classroom duties. At a majority of institutions, however, professors must learn how to divide themselves like Gaul into three parts, research and publication, classroom teaching, and institutional or community service. They are held accountable in the three areas.

In institutions relying on the publish-or-perish formula as the touchstone of a professor's merit for promotion and tenure, the practice tends to deteriorate to a mere count of articles published. At one college the publishing pressure-cooker propels anxious teachers at year's end to pile their rejection slips on the department chairman's desk as evidence of their efforts to fulfill this obligation.

Some institutions solicit opinions of a professor from his peers in the same field in other institutions. Mostly, however, the opinions are sought from his department colleagues. Sometimes the department chairman is queried and the professor being evaluated may be asked for a self-evaluation.

The cupboard is practically bare of standardized research instruments with which to assess research and publication. Thus, under the circumstances, some institutions have procreated checklists to help in the judging.

Form 14.
RESEARCH/PUBLICATION WORK
FACULTY SELF-APPRAISAL

Faculty member _____

Dept. _____Date _____

This faculty self-appraisal form has been devised to facilitate the process of up-grading professional effectiveness.

Please do not let modesty prevent you from being explicit about your assets. Equally important, try to be just as candid about your short-comings.

Please rate your performance by drawing a circle around the number that most closely expresses your view.

		Low				High	Don't Know
1.	How do you rate the importance of this research study/publication to your field?	1	2	3	4	5	X
2.	How do colleagues within the department rate the contribution of this research study/publication to your field?	1	2	3	4	5	X
3.	How do you rate the quality of this publication?	1	2	3	4	5	X
4.	Has this research study/publication made you a more effective teacher?	1	2	3	4	5	X
5.	Has this research study/publication interfered with your teaching responsibilities?	1	2	3	4	5	X
6.	Do you seek assistance from faculty colleagues in your research/publication activities?	1	2	3	4	5	X

7. Compared to others in the de-   1 2 3 4 5   X
partment, how would you rate
your research/publication performance? (Please elaborate)

_____

_____

_____

_____

8. Describe the nature of your research study/publication.

_____

_____

_____

_____

To be genuinely helpful, peer rating instruments should include some specific questions, a point-range scale of perhaps 1-5 or 1-7, and some questions calling for open-end answers. The format should be simple and the instructions clear (see Forms 14, 15, 16 for examples). Miller (1972) adds the suggestion that books, monographs, special reports, book chapters, articles each be dealt with by separate forms.

A few typical questions for peer and self-appraisal follow:
Peer Appraisal
1. As a colleague in the department, how do you rate the adequacy of the research design?
2. As a colleague outside the institution, how do you rate the importance of the research (or nonresearch) study to your discipline?
3. How is the research related to this professor's teaching responsibility?
4. If a nonresearch study, how is it related to this professor's teaching responsibility?
5. As a colleague outside the institution, how do you rate the periodical which published the study?
Self-Appraisal

1. Briefly describe the nature of your research.

2. What is the importance of this research to your field?

3. If your study was not research-based, explain briefly its importance to your field.

4. If you were to do the research over again, would you do it the same way? Differently? How?

5. How do you rate the quality of the publication(s) in which your article(s) appeared?

6. How do you rate your overall performance in research and publication?

Form 15.

SELF-REPORT ON RESEARCH/PUBLICATION WORK

Faculty member _____ Dept. _____ Date _____

Directions: Please fill out one form for each unit of work. Check appropriate answers and write "n/a" for questions that are not applicable.

Work Type:

____abstract	____case	____occasional paper
____article	____chapter in book	____research paper
____book	____comment	____paper in proceedings
____book of readings	____handbook	____technical report
____book review	____monograph	____translation
	____other _____	_____

Bibliographic Listing:

(Include author(s) name; title of work; periodical name, volume and number; publication date and place; and publisher.)

_____

_____

_____

Your Role:

____sole investigator	____project director
____principle investigator	____contributor

Was the research/publication funded? _____

If yes, indicate source of funding and amount: _____

_____

_____

_____

Note: If this work has received professional recognition, please provide specifics on reverse side of paper.

Source: Adopted from Flewellen (1975).

It is essential that the form allow sufficient space for detailed responses, and it is a good idea to allow extra space for free comments. No one can reasonably expect thoughtful and fair colleague appraisal unless all the material evidence is available for on-the-spot examination. It is useful if the colleague can discuss the research first-hand with the professor who did it. To judge publications, they must be at hand.

It goes without saying that only peers qualified by personal and close examination of all relevant material should be asked to fill out a rating instrument. To do less would invite inequity into the instrument. In fact, it may be astute to ask each peer to spell out the reasons for his judgments.

At some institutions the professor is allowed to select his evaluators from a list submitted to him. This practice allows the professor latitude to position peers more intimately familiar with his work to judge it. But care must be exercised to guard against bias, for or against.

Faculty confidence in the rating forms and their administration is the key to faculty acceptance of the evaluation program. In the absence of confidence the program is foredoomed. And that confidence cannot be created overnight. It is developed step-by-step by planning the program's construction jointly by the administration and faculty. There is no short cut to institutional integrity.

Additional problems inherent in programs evaluating research and publication, as viewed by Flewellen (1972), are:

1. The great mass of information to be obtained and processed.
2. Devising appropriate evaluative instruments.
3. Recording the data in useful form.
4. Learning to use the data properly.
5. Preparing reports to the professor, department chairman, and dean.

Overriding these problems, warns Flewellen, and at the heart of the program is the selection of criteria for the appraisal and assigning appropriate weight to each.

At the University of Georgia, in the College of Business Administration, of which Flewellen is the academic dean, a remarkably comprehensive system was devised which assigned weights to 111 different kinds of publications. The system was so ambitiously comprehensive and detailed that it became administratively unwieldly and drew a drumfire of faculty criticism and overt opposition. Commenced in the early 1970's it was dropped in 1977.

It possibly proved that an evaluation program seemingly utterly objective and quantified nonetheless retained arbitrary elements that ultimately destroyed the program. The intense desire to recognize value only in judgments based on objective criteria left no room for human judgment. Perhaps the human touch with all its subjective frailty, like Prometheus' touch, brings life to human endeavors, even an evaluation system.

Form 16.
PEER APPRAISAL OF RESEARCH/PUBLICATION WORK

Faculty member _____

Dept. _____ Date _____

Appraiser _____ Title _____

Please indicate your appraisal of the faculty member named above in regard to the following factors by drawing a circle around the number that most closely expresses your view.

		Low		High	Don't Know
1.	How do you rate the adequacy of the research design (if applicable)?	1 2 3 4		5	X
2.	How do colleagues outside the department rate the importance of the research study/publication?	1 2 3 4		5	X
3.	Is the research study/publication closely related to the faculty member's area of teaching responsibility?	1 2 3 4		5	X
4.	How do you rate the quality of this publication?	1 2 3 4		5	X
5.	Was appropriate professional time and effort spent on this research study/publication?	1 2 3 4		5	X

6. Compared to others in the de-   1 2 3 4 5   X
   partment, how do you rate the
   research/publication performance of this faculty member?

7. What is this faculty member's greatest strength with regard to
   research/publication? (Please elaborate)

_____

_____

_____

8. What are his most serious short-comings? (Please elaborate)

_____

_____

_____

_____

9. Additional comments. (Use reverse side if necessary)

_____

_____

_____

Chapter 9

Models of Evaluation

Those who do not learn from their mistakes are doomed to repeat them, the philosopher Santayana warns. Similarly, institutions of higher learning which have decided to embark on a faculty evaluation program, or further to develop an existing program, can avoid many mistakes by learning from the experience of other institutions. There is no special virtue in repeating errors.

Care must be taken, of course, to adapt the borrowed evaluation model to local needs. The data sources, criteria, and scoring weights, for example, must be congenial to such needs. But the point needs underscoring that relatively successful evaluation models are operating on many campuses and are available for the asking.

THE TEACHING PORTFOLIO

It is customary at most colleges and universities for each faculty member to provide an annual update of his teaching, research, publication and institutional service. But the teaching component is generally nothing more than a numerical listing of the teacher's courses and students. This most casual appraisal of teaching offers no insights for the faculty activity report, which plays a hefty role in tenure, promotion and merit pay decisions. It would be difficult to advance an argument against the introduction of a more substantive appraisal than a simple numerical listing.

Including student ratings is necessary but not sufficient for a proper appraisal. Needed also are corollary data in part to provide information which students are unlikely to have or be able to make good judgment about, and in part to take account of teaching which takes place outside the classroom. One source of such corollary data is the teaching portfolio.

Knapper (1978, p.1124) describes the teaching portfolio thus:

It would provide a short (two or three page) description that serves to accurately convey the scope and type of the faculty member's teaching endeavours. Just as a list of publications is usually selective, so too would the teaching dossier (portfolio) contain only some of the instructor's accomplishments; just as statements concerning scholarship and research in a curriculum vitae must be supportable by more complete evidence (published papers or even the actual research data), so the claims made in the teaching dossier (portfolio) should ultimately be supportable by fuller empirical evidence if and when this is required.

The teaching portfolio is a novel concept with minimal experience in the most useful and effective formats. One caution in its use: it should be tailored to the needs of the faculty member, the department and institution.

An approach at the University of Massachusetts is to encourage faculty to develop and monitor a special folder documenting efforts to improve teaching. A model portfolio, suggest Melnick and Adams (1975), might include videotapes of classroom teaching, appraisal of teaching performance by selected students, appraisal by colleagues of student evaluations, and details of relevant inservice courses and/or workshops attended.

Melnick and Adams recommend that not only each faculty member should maintain a portfolio but also the department chairman for each faculty member. In the chairman's individual teacher portfolio would rest relevant notes on the teacher by administrators, colleagues, students. Those who penned the notes would be required to sign them. This would mute the anonymous antagonist, lend credence to the notes, and most important permit the teacher to respond to them. The chairman's portfolio thus would be inhospitable to rumor, invective and blue-sky praise.

Another approach is suggested in *Faculty Development in a Time of Retrenchment* (1975), published by *Change Magazine*. It urges the creation of on-campus institutes as generators of factual material on the teaching competency of graduate students and nontenured faculty. The institutes would gauge teaching performance for the record. They would arrange for teams of classroom observers, from the same or another institution, to describe the teaching methods and gauge the teaching mastery. Recommended are several observations by several observers as a safeguard against possible individual bias for or against a personality or teaching style.

At Evergreen State College (Washington), as one of the conditions for reappointment, each faculty member is required to maintain a portfolio of factual evidence of work at and for the college during the contract period. The Evergreen Faculty Handbook (section 4.400, p. 3) notes that the portfolio is considered "the principal documentary evidence for a thorough evaluation by the Deans and the principal source for determining satisfactory performance in the criteria for reappointment or non-appointment."

The portfolio is expected to contain:

1. The faculty member's self-evaluation and the dean's evaluation from the previous year.
2. All evaluations by faculty colleagues.
3. All evaluations by the faculty member of his colleagues.
4. All evaluations by staff members.
5. All evaluations by the faculty member of the staff.
6. All student evaluations.
7. All evaluations by the faculty member of his students, both transcript and in-house evaluations.
8. Copies of group or individual contracts between the faculty member and his students.
9. A comprehensive self-evaluation of the past year, after examination of all the material in the portfolio, including successes, disappointments and planned areas targeted for improvement.

Each year an Evergreen State College academic dean reviews each faculty portfolio and simultaneously his own portfolio is reviewed by the faculty member. The dean and the faculty member then exchange responses to the other's evaluation which are also included in their portfolios.

Knapper (op. cit.) suggests as a logical first step in the development of a teaching portfolio a clear, concise statement on the agreements, formal or informal, between the teacher and the chairman or academic dean on the teaching responsibilities and indices of teaching mastery. The statement should consist of several parts. First, it should contain such data as the number of courses taught, the kind or level of courses, the yardsticks employed to measure student progress, and specifics on teaching methods and content. Second, it should contain facts on teaching duties relating to all courses and generally include such items as:

1. Student enrollment.
2. Is the course required or elective?
3. Is it upper or lower division?
4. A brief description of the teaching method (lecture, discussion, seminar, independent study, computer-assisted) and the methods of examining student learning. Copies of classroom examinations are desired.
5. A description of any course development such as revision of course material.

6. Copies of handouts, outlines, problem sets and innovative student assignments.

7. If relevant, responsibility for laboratory work and noncredit seminars.

Since the supervision of graduate and honors students is a teaching responsibility, Knapper suggests that mention of this fact be included in teaching portfolios of students who successfully complete their theses. Also, students whose later academic achievements can be traced back to the supervising teacher, should have that fact noted in the teacher's portfolio.

The third component of the statement should deal with informal teaching activities. These include tutorials (individual and group), keeping up-to-date in curriculum changes, offering sound advice to students on both academic and personal problems, serving on teaching/learning committees and in a learning resource center, attending summer research institutes, serving on regional accreditation teams, preparing and submitting research proposals to funding agencies, participating in state and national academic conferences, dealing with textbook and equipment representatives.

Documenting Teaching Activities

How is effective teaching documented? In the U.S., student ratings play a predominant role. In a less stellar role are:

1. Results of colleague classroom observation.
2. Colleagues in team teaching.
3. Student examination performance.
4. Alumni opinions.
5. Self-evaluation.
6. Comments of colleagues teaching the same students in subsequent courses.
7. Teaching materials (syllabus, readings, examinations and grading, teaching methods, course objectives, homework assignments, handouts, lecture notes).
8. Comments of current employers of former students.
9. Evaluations by department chairman and dean.
10. Grade distributions.
11. Indications that student career choices were properly guided by the teacher.
12. Student interviews prior to graduation.
13. Student enrollment in elective courses taught by the instructor.
14. Awards or other recognition for quality teaching.

15. Invitations to other campuses to demonstrate effective instruction methods, or participation in teaching/learning symposia.

16. Participation in state and national conferences on the improvement of teaching and learning.

17. Colleague ratings on the instructor's scholarly competency.

18. Audio or visual tapes of a classroom session.

19. Student scores on standardized examinations.

20. Participation in campus teaching improvement center.

Gaining Faculty Acceptance of the Teaching Portfolio

Even on campuses of higher education there is an indecent amount of xenophobia toward strangers bearing new ideas. The teaching portfolio is no exception; some faculty members have taken to the barricades to resist the incursion of the teaching portfolio. The antagonism grows out of uncertainty and a tinge of fear that somehow the teacher is threatened. Thus, it is the height of prudence to discuss the portfolio program openly, carefully, candidly, before its implementation. The utility of the teaching portfolio as an additional, not replacement, source of information on teaching performance must be made clear.

When the program gains a measure of faculty acceptance, conducting dry runs will tend to improve the mechanics of gathering and organizing the portfolio material. The dry runs will also tend to lower the level of faculty anxiety. It may require a year, even two, before program bugs are ironed out and faculty acceptance is achieved. Follow-up procedures to evaluate the portfolio system itself, should be spelled out.

A final word of caution: the teaching portfolio is hardly a cure-all for the manifold problems implicit in faculty evaluation. At most, it is a helpful tool. As Knapper (op. cit., p. 1128) points out, its effectiveness depends on how well the teacher documents his case and on the acceptability of the program by the faculty. The portfolio, he warns, "cannot gloss over terrible teaching." But it is a way of "documenting good teaching and hence gaining for its compiler the appropriate credit."

MERIT INCREASE AWARDS—FORDHAM UNIVERSITY, FACULTY OF BUSINESS

Selecting faculty as deserving of merit increase awards has always been a hazardous, if necessary, higher education program. Many professors support the principle of merit pay but fall out on the deciding criteria. Others insist that they are the only accurate judges of their teaching performances. Still others argue that faculty evaluation is an infringement on academic freedom and support across-the-board salary increments or a percentage increment depending on professorial rank.

Traditionally, in higher education, recognition is accorded to professors whose activities, in the administration's judgment, warrant it. The First Report of the Assembly on University Goals and Governance of the American Academy of Arts and Sciences (1971, p. 17), in support of the tradition, advises that "the principle of differential rewards for merit in teaching and scholarship...should not be tampered with...."

How to construct an appraisal system for merit increases that is, at once, comprehensive, individualized, fair? How to devise reliable criteria?

What follows are the merit award guidelines adopted in the Spring of 1979 by the Fordham University Faculty of Business. They may make for useful reading and discussion at universities now grappling with the problem.

1.   Each faculty member may elect not to be evaluated for merit increases without any prejudice regarding future tenure and promotion decisions.

2.   Each faculty member considered for merit increase will be evaluated on his teaching, service and research, with equal weight assigned to each criterion.

3.   Each faculty member requesting merit evaluation shall submit a copy of the standard University Activity Report and, if desired, an individual supplement to the Merit Increase Awards Coordinating Committee by a fixed date announced at least several weeks in advance.

4.   Activity Reports shall be in the following format:
   (a) Research/publications: Prioritized by contributions to the University and annotated as necessary.
   (b) University/Community service: Same as above.
   (c) Teaching: Course names and numbers, number of students. Also included for each faculty member will be a summary of student course evaluations for the prior 12 months.
   Evaluation will be based on Activity Reports.

5.   Merit candidates will be rated separately for the three criteria. Raw scores will be summed then divided by the number of non-blank votes and the three resulting averages will be summed and ranked for purposes of merit nomination.

6.   Within two or three weeks of the due date for the Activity Reports copies of all materials will be available for examination. Each eligible full-time faculty member is expected to review this material *before* the balloting meeting. For security, all materials will

be controlled by the Dean's secretaries.

7. Merit candidates shall be rated by secret ballots physically presented and counted at an open meeting specifically called for this purpose. The eligible full-time faculty members may submit their ballots which must be in sealed, double envelopes signed on the outer envelope. The signed envelopes shall be opened and filed for future reference. The inner envelopes shall be combined, opened together, and counted. The suggested date for this open meeting is the last Friday of the May examination period.

8. To determine the eligibility of the full-time faculty, a ballot shall be prepared in advance listing all candidates for merit increases, and this ballot shall be submitted to the Associate Academic Vice President for validation. Also to be included will be a list of full-time faculty not eligible for merit increase.

9. Balloting results shall be submitted to the Dean. Following the Dean's review, the results (including scores) of those receiving merit increases shall be promulgated to the faculty. The Dean has the right to reject faculty nominations with an explanation to the faculty. If a nomination is rejected the vacancy shall be filled by the next person beyond the cut-off point. The Dean's decision is final.

10. All ballots, Activity Reports, and scores shall be retained in the Dean's office for six months. Names, scores, Activity Reports, and vote summary of those receiving awards shall be available to all faculty members, who shall have access to their own ballots, scores, and relative rank.

11. The size of the merit increment awarded to a faculty member shall normally be limited to the minimun allocation. A discretionary fund will be available to the Dean for special awards he may wish to make. Each special award must be accompanied by an explanation by the Dean to the faculty. The Dean's discretionary fund shall be determined by dividing 85 percent of the total merit increase pool by the minimum allocation and the result subtracted from the total merit increase pool. The number of awards made by the faculty will thus be equal to the rounded down number defined above. This number determines the cut-off point in the rankings. In the event of a tie at the bottom, the Dean will decide.

12. The Dean's discretionary fund shall be used to promote unusually meritorious service.

13. In rating the three criteria a standard scale shall be applied by those eligible to participate in the evaluations. A seven-point scale is suggested where seven corresponds to exceptional performance. In computing scores a blank will be considered as an abstention for determining average scores.

148

FACULTY EVALUATION: A QUANTITY AND QUALITY MODEL

Most colleges and universities, in considering a faculty member's workload and evaluation, try to define what does or should count. They try to fix professional responsibilities in terms of maximum cost-benefits to the institutions. Thus, all professors are squeezed into the same Procrustean bed. Personal skills, values, interests, attitudes are viewed as irrelevant in the assessment of faculty performance. And a 26-year-old assistant professor finds himself judged by the same standards as a 60-year-old full professor.

Moreover, few institutions have defined the evaluative criteria with enough precision and specificity. Nor have they come up with clean judgments on the relative importance of teaching, research/publication, and institutional/community service. The inevitable result is confusion in the minds of professors as to how their performances will be judged.

Buhl and Lane (1977) have tried to dispel the fog by developing a model to account for both quantity and quality factors in teaching performance. An example of the model for one academic division is offered in abbreviated form as Figure 3. The first step toward implementation is for the division head and campus administrators to agree upon the model's broad categories and the number of units to be allocated to each category. The second step is for the faculty in each division to propose the unit allocations in each category. The job of assigning weights to teaching-related activities, as a percentage of all their professional responsibilities, is left to the faculty members themselves. In this example, it is 80 percent.

Teaching and other responsibilities (I,A,B,) are negotiated at the beginning of the academic year by the department chairman and each faculty member. Each professor's quality points are added to, or subtracted from, the quantity total at the end of the year. The example is based on a quarterly approach.

Buhl and Lane see several unique advantages in their model:

1. It is simple, understandable, manageable. Summed over the normal three-term (quarter) academic year, the unit credits may range from about 95 to 125, making possible a meaningful assessment of performance differences.

2. It is easily adaptable by other institutions. The approximately four-to-one ratio of "instructional responsibilities" to "other responsibilities" can be adjusted in accordance with each institution's gauge of their relative importance. Similarly, the relative importance of quantity and quality can also be adjusted by each institution.

Figure 3.
The Abbreviated Model for One Division

I. Quantitative Component

   A. Instructional Responsibilities

      1. Number of contact hours (1 contact hour = 1-1/2 units)
      2. Number of preparations (1 = 0 units, 2 = 8 units, 3 = 12 units)
      3. Evening or Saturday classes (2 - 6 units)
      4. Class size (150 students = 1 unit, 200 = 2 units, 300 = 3 units)
      5. New course (1.5 - 3 units)

          Instructional responsibilities total   *30*

   B. Other Responsibilities

      1. Department/Division Committees (1 - 3 units)
      2. Club Advisor (.5 - 1 unit)
      3. Work on departmental curriculum (1 - 2 units)
      4. Recruiting and Placement activity (.5 - 1 unit)
      5. Attending workshops on teaching (.5 - 2 units)
      6. Preparing new courses (1 - 2 units)
      7. Attending professional workshops (.5 - 2 units)

          Other responsibilities total   7
          Quantitative total   37

II. Qualitative Component
   A. Instruction

      1. Student Ratings

+2	+1	0	-1	-2
decile ranking above 85% or a decile ranking of 70–80% and documentation that evaluative data is being used for improvement	decile ranking of 70–85% or a decile ranking of 30–70% and documentation that evaluative data is being used for improvement	decile ranking of 30–70% or a decile ranking of 10–30% and documentation that evaluative data is being used for improvement	decile ranking of 10–30% or a decile ranking of 10% and documentation that evaluative data is being used for improvement	decile ranking below 10% and no evidence that evaluation is being used for improvement

150

2. Course Design

+2	+1	0	-1	-2
all courses are well designed conformity with some model described in the literature on teaching and learning	3/4 of all courses are well designed in conformity with some model described in the literature on teaching and learning	at least 1/2 but not greater than 3/4 of all courses are well designed in conformity with some model described in the literature on teaching and learning	1/4 but not greater than 1/2 of all courses are well designed in conformity with some model described in the literature on teaching and learning	less than 1/4 are well designed in conformity with some model described in the literature on teaching and learning

B. Institutional Service

+1	0	-1
documented evidence that the individual discharged all assigned non-instructional tasks responsibly and at least one of them, by consensus of those affected, in an exceptional manner	documented evidence that the individual discharged all assigned non-instructional tasks responsibly	documented evidence that the individual failed to discharge or discharged irresponsibly one or more assigned non-instructional tasks

Instructional responsibilities total (30)
+ Other responsibilities total (7)

Quantitative total 37
+ Qualitative total (±5)

EVALUATION TOTAL 32 to 42

Source: Buhl and Lane (1977)

3. It acknowledges differences in instructional responsibilities between faculty members and bestows credit for such added responsibilities as service on department/institution committees, advising students, and participation in academic conferences.

4. Its premise is that most professors perform acceptably most of the time. It measures performance above and below the acceptable level.

5. It does not split hairs on the worth of contributions by faculty members. Thus, it avoids the possible personal biases pro and con concerning methodology or teaching style. The model works to comfort the security of the 75 percent of the faculty whose performance is "acceptable" and thus brightens the entire prospect of faculty acceptance. In turn, this acts as a positive impulse to improve performance.

6. It is based on a variety of informational sources on teaching effectiveness. Although the example uses student ratings and course design, other sources are classroom visitation, self-appraisal, review of instructional materials, level of student learning.

7. It entices faculty participation at the grass-roots level. The divisional faculty (or academic unit) defines the categories of activities, determines what does and does not count, fixes the weighting, decides on the qualitative values. Then, when the system is in place, each faculty member negotiates on his own professional responsibilities, both quantity and quality.

FACULTY EVALUATION—THE AMERICAN UNIVERSITY, SCHOOL OF BUSINESS ADMINISTRATION

The American University (Washington, D.C.), like other colleges and universities struggling to raise income and lower costs, has tightened the funds available for salary increases and simultaneously tightened the requisites for promotion in rank.

To cope with the unhappy situation, the School of Business (SBA) has constructed a cost-benefit analysis in the evaluation of faculty performance. As drafted by Dean Herbert Striner, the system was presented, debated, modified, in a series of open faculty meetings. The faculty members were kept informed and actively engaged as the system evolved. The administration was receptive to faculty suggestions and, as a result, received considerable faculty support. The system (see Figure 4) measures four areas of faculty performance: (1) teaching effectiveness, (2) professional development, (3) service, (4) special incidents.

(1) *Teaching effectiveness.* Since most of the faculty expressed opposition to classroom visits, the practice was banned from the evaluation system. Self-evaluation also fell victim to faculty opposition on the ground that it presented the faculty with an awful Hobson's choice. Revelation of a vital teaching weakness could result in denial of an intended promotion or salary jump, and nonrevelation meant tampering with the truth. Teaching effectiveness is based therefore on:

A. An appraisal of the faculty member's innovations in curriculum development, experiments in teaching, and other actions to improve instruction. Each item is separately evaluated.

B. The accumulated weighted average of six questions extracted from the university's Student Evaluation Questionnaire given in the fall and spring semesters. The six questions and their point values are the following:

1) In my opinion, the instructor presents the material:

effectively	4
about average	3
not very effectively	2
very ineffectively	1

2) The availability of the instructor outside class, including announced office hours, is:

very good	5
good	4
about average	3
fair	2
poor	1

3) My overall evaluation of the instructor is that he/she is:

one of the best	5
better than most	4
about average	3
worse than most	2
one of the worst	1

4) Compared to other college courses you have taken, this course is:

one of the best	5
better than most	4
about average	3
worse than most	2
one of the worst	1

5) Compared to other college courses you have taken, how much do you feel you have learned from this course:

considerably more	5
somewhat more	4
about the same	3
somewhat less	2
considerably less	1

6) Compared to other college courses you have had, how would you rate the overall difficulty of the course:

very easy	1
easy	2
about the same	3
difficult	4
very difficult	5

By averaging the responses to each question the professor's overall classroom effectiveness is appraised, and to avoid the effect of a skewed return from one class, the responses from all the professor's classes are counted.

(2) *Professional development.* The measurement of professional development is both quantitative and qualitative. Publications are rated by type: 5 points for a book, 4 for a chapter, 3 for a journal

article, 1 for a book review. Journals are rated from zero to three depending on reputation and circulation. Single authors receive full credit, coauthors partial credit. Only original work receives credit recognition.

Research is evaluated in terms of time and sponsorship. Sponsored research earns 3 points, self-funded research 1 point. Research leading to publication picks up no additional points beyond that allotted to the publication.

Program appearances and participation in executive-management programs, or extension and public service activities, are awarded a modest one-tenth of a point. In the absence of a travel budget, membership in professional societies and attendance at meetings count for naught. Honors and special recognition from professional associations are evaluated individually.

(3) *Service*. Service to the University, School and students weighs in according to the activity. Every SBA and University-wide committee, for example, is rated from zero to five depending on the time committed and the value to the University. The committee chairman evaluates each committee member's contribution in quantitative and qualitative terms. Other service-related activity, for example playing a key role in a campus organization, is separately evaluated. One-half point is awarded for supervising an independent study course, or for membership on a dissertation committee.

Classroom teaching is the most highly prized component of faculty performance. Professional development comes in second, service third. This priority is reflected in the points awarded to each category which are multiplied by descending weights as follows:

Teaching effectiveness point total	$\times$ 1.0	= _____
Professional development point total	$\times$ .6	= _____
Service point total	$\times$ .4	= _____

Subtotal _____

(4) *Special incidents*. The subtotal can be slightly raised or lowered by the Dean. It can be elevated for outstanding service, commendations, or simply to adjust a salary inequity. It can be lowered for persistent negative evaluations by students or faculty, or repeated reprimands.

Application of the data. The process calls for each faculty member to complete data sheets and spell out his activities during the calendar year. The sheets then go to the Dean's office where point scores are calculated by academic rank. Next, each professor's

154

Figure 4.
The American University
Components of the SBA Faculty Evaluation Instrument

Teaching Effectiveness

1. Accumulated weighted average of 6 questions taken from The American University Student Evaluation Questionnaires from the Fall and Spring semesters.

2. Assessment of the faculty member's involvement in innovative curriculum development, experimentation in teaching methods, and other meaningful efforts to improve the instructional program during the base year.

    - each item is evaluated individually on its own merits

Professional Development

1. Publications during the base year

    - (weighting from type of publication) (weight of journal) (# of authors)

2. Noteworthy research in base year

    - 3 points for sponsored research, 1 point for self-funded

3. Noteworthy program appearances during the base year

    - 1/10 point per appearance

4. Involvement in executive-management development programs, extension, and public service activities

    - 1/10 point per day or fraction of day

5. Honors and special recognition from professional associations during the base year

    - each item is evaluated individually on its own merits

6. Other activities contributing significantly to professional development

    - each item is evaluated individually on its own merits

Service

1. Number of dissertations or independent studies supervised

    - 1/2 point for each

2. SBA committee assignments during the base year

    - (weight of committee) (chairman's evaluation) (1/2 - if only 1 semester)

3. TAU committee assignments during the base year

    - (weight of committee) (1/2 - if only 1 semester)

4. Other service-related activities such as key roles held in other campus organizations, etc.

    - each item is evaluated individually on its own merits

Source: Striner (1979)

155

percentage is multiplied by the total number of dollars available for salary increases at that rank. For example, if an assistant professor receives 45 points out of a total of 450 points available for all assistant professors, he would be entitled to 10 percent of the funds set aside for salary increases.

Then, tables and bar graphs are prepared which graphically illustrate the point totals for each faculty member for teaching effectiveness, professional development, service, and special incidents. The point totals are ranked for each faculty grade and for the faculty as a whole. Each faculty member receives his personal results and is also handed a copy of the results for the entire faculty. The faculty remains anonymous, no names appear.

This appraisal system tends to pinpoint any faculty weakness in the separate areas. Once identified, the department chairman can discuss the weakness and in concert with the professor come up with a workable remedy.

Not only is the system successful in more equitably distributing salary increases, but Dean Striner reports (1979) that the system is also being extended to determine eligibility for promotion in rank. Although Dean Striner acknowledges that the system "works beautifully and is highly effective," he cautions that the results so far can best be labeled approximations.

As with many assessments, this one contains some criteria that lend themselves to easy quantification and others that are more defiant of the analyst. A subjective (read arbitrary) element comes to the analyst's aid in overcoming the defiance. It thereby weakens the system. The clear advantage of the American University system is the consistency with which it is applied to all faculty members. "Consistency," says Striner, "is the key to the system."

Is the system accepted by the faculty in the School of Business? Yes, says the Dean. The majority accept the system as comprehensive and equitable. It takes into account the faculty member's individual contributions.

Dean Striner cautions institutions on the brink of adapting the system. Be certain, he says, to win faculty support before implementation. Hold open faculty forums. Explain completely, candidly, disarmingly the inner workings and purposes of the system. And do not complicate and encumber the system so that it becomes unwieldy and falls of its own weight. Guard its comprehensiveness and simplicity.

Beyond the cautions, the system needs no further justification for it seems to work.

Chapter 10

Guide to Successful Faculty Evaluation

It is a truism that colleges and universities aspire to, and would enjoy nothing better than faculty excellence. What prevents it? Everyone wants it, why isn't it achieved? First of all, faculty members face frustration as they try to juggle teaching, research, publication, public service, professional society membership, student advising, campus committees, to the satisfaction of their institution and academic discipline. They also have their own varied personal interests to pursue. Second of all, because evaluative criteria are general and therefore hard to pin down, at too many institutions the professors operate in the semi-dark about how their performance will be evaluated. The inevitable result: an unfortunate mixture of faculty confusion, disillusion, friction.

What can be done? How can institutions develop flexible, comprehensive and patently fair systems of faculty appraisal? How can all this be served up to the faculty?

The following guidelines are offered as therapy for ailing appraisal systems.

Purpose of System. The overriding purpose of evaluation is clearly to improve the teaching program, to move toward faculty excellence. While this is the professed purpose at most institutions, at least in theory, it tends to fall far short of accomplishment in practice. The practice needs to catch up with the theory.

Another predominant purpose of evaluation is to prepare the rationale for salary, retention, promotion and tenure decisions. In recent years, in a period of economic stress, this purpose has captured the lion's share of campus attention. Many institutions have developed separate procedures for these two evaluative purposes.

Open Communication. No evaluation program stands much chance to succeed unless it is candidly and completely explained to the faculty and administration, and is understood and accepted by both. Any sugarcoating, obfuscation or sly maneuvering in the explanatory process or its implementation virtually dooms the program to failure.

Program components and practices must be openly and democratically arrived at and must be widely publicized throughout the institution. Faculty forums or open hearings are particularly useful when draft documents are being considered. To assure thoughtful faculty consideration, the documents should be distributed in advance. At the hearings, each evaluation proposal should be openly discussed, and the intellectual atmosphere needs to be one of persuasion and understanding, not of raised voices or attempts to win debating points. Inviting student government leaders and faculty senate officers as attendees will help demonstrate the openness of the hearings. Regular progress reports as the evaluative system develops should be forwarded to all faculty members. The names of faculty members serving on evaluation committees must be public information.

Open communication means that every faculty member knows accurately and completely the criteria, standards and evidence needed for salary increase, promotion, tenure. It also means complete knowledge of institutional policies and procedures in performance evaluation. In summary, the professors must know what is expected of them and exactly how their performance will be judged. Open communication also demands prompt feedback to the professors of the results of their evaluations.

Faculty Involvement. To make the evaluation system acceptable means that the professors must have a strong hand in its development. Each discipline may require separate standards and methods, but for accuracy's sake they must be reviewed by a higher body, perhaps by the faculty senate, academic dean, or board of trustees. And above all, the professors must be directly involved with developing and running the program. The professors must never lose the feeling that they are in control of their destiny.

If the professors actively partake in its development, they will "own" the program that ultimately emerges and more readily accept its implementation. Those whose opinions are solicited and given serious and respectful consideration, and when feasible incorporated into the program, will more likely consider the end product fair and meaningful.

Campus Influentials. Every college and university has faculty influentials whose support is mandatory if the evaluation program is not to succumb. This handful of faculty heavyweights is needed in the administration's corner. Convinced of its worth, they can help bring success to the program. It is practical to court their support.

Administrative Backing. Another group whose support is vital to the evaluation program is the administrators. They are trained to break log-jams, to offer acceptable compromises, and to lend the force of their office to publicize the program on the campus. They must not only be committed to the program but also see that it operates effectively. They must a) give the faculty the lead in the

158

program's development and implementation; b) provide the necessary resources; c) avoid handing down the program even when initiated by the administration; d) support the program with enough enthusiasm to help it overcome week-by-week obstacles.

Multi-source Information. A common mistake is to accept the student evaluation of a professor's classroom teaching as representing the total professor. This approach obviously fails to consider the multi-facets of faculty responsibility (researcher, student advisor, committee member, etc.) to say nothing of professorial aspects of which students may be completely unaware or incapable of sound judgments. Collateral information from other sources is essential if the total professor is to emerge in the evaluation process.

Just as some student evaluations may not fairly represent the professor, so too some colleague evaluations may depart from objectivity. Some procedures like videotaping of classes may not be acceptable to the professor. And his teaching performance on any given day may not represent his teaching as a whole. To meet these and other objections, the assessment of teaching performance must draw on many resources to come out reasonably accurate.

Each source of information, student, colleague, administrator, self-assessment, offers important but limited insights. No single source is enough for tenure, promotion, retention decisions. Combining the sources is to produce a three-dimensional professor, not a cardboard figure.

What information can be expected from each source?

From students: an appraisal of classroom teaching skills and the structure of the course (materials, exams, papers), work load, course difficulty level, professor-class interaction, professor-individual student interaction, student advising, organization, displayed interest in teaching, clarity of presentation, dynamism, enthusiasm.

From faculty peers: an appraisal of the appropriateness of course and instructional objectives, a review of teaching materials (assignments, hand-outs, tests, papers, projects, textbooks), mastery and currency of subject matter, research activity and professional recognition, participation in the academic community, student relations, displayed concern for teaching, research, service.

From administrators: an appraisal of course load and other responsibilities, course enrollment factors, service to the institution and community, long-range evaluation and discernible improvement patterns, marketability of the course and department.

From the professor: a self-appraisal of teaching and other responsibilities, representative illustrative material, evidence of accomplishments, course and instructional objectives, student advising, committee memberships, service to the institution and community.

Weighting in advance the relative importance of each activity of the total professor, and applying the multi-source approach with its internal system of checks and balances, produces, or is more likely to produce, the true value of the professor to the institution and to the community.

Importance of Criteria. Whatever the system, it is critical that institutions make explicit the criteria used for administrative decisions. Styles of governance may differ, but the hallmark of institutional criteria, jointly developed by administration and faculty, is specificity. It is prudent to allow for individual differences in the development of faculty criteria, so long as these differences can be tolerated by departmental and institutional goals. In general, it is best to develop criteria within the smallest practical unit. Infrequently, it will be the entire institution; generally, it will be a department or a group of departments with dominant similarities. Curiously, and regrettably, many institutions center their attention on fine points of methodology rather than on the criteria. As a result, the important question is diverted to whether the colleague visits a classroom by invitation or by chance. Lost in the debate is what is to be observed in the classroom. It is necessary always to keep in mind what is important.

Faculty Resistance. The introduction of any new program is likely to bring out imagined and real objections from some faculty members. It would only serve to compound the problem to apply administrative muscle to the resistance. Experience has provided more effective approaches.

First, spread the word about the proposed evaluation program, and be candid and truthful. Scrupulous attention must be paid to campus protocol; use the proper communication channels to collect and distribute information.

Second, encourage the faculty senate to hold open forums at which members of the evaluation committee can answer questions and record suggested changes. The committee must be completely familiar with all aspects of the proposed program, its consequences and implications, and must be conversant with current research findings in evaluation.

Third, consider the evaluation program as experimental. Neither the form of the instruments nor the administrative procedures should be considered as etched in stone.

Fourth, protect the privacy of the professor. Prohibit the public distribution of a professor's evaluation without the permission of the professor. It will help defuse the opposition. It also helps to invite each faculty member to fix the weights of his index of appraisal according to his own teaching objectives. Many an opponent has thus been converted to supporter.

Fifth, allow one or two years for the process of acceptance and implementation. During this period, draft documents are carefully prepared, freely discussed, modified when needed. All parts of the program need not be in place before implementation. The quest for perfection may be endless, a Jason's search for the golden fleece. Don't stall the program in a futile search for perfection. Start the program incrementally and be flexible to modification as it develops.

Sixth, apply gentlemanly and understanding pressure on resistance points; try to grasp the reasons for the resistance and offer responsive answers.

Seventh, don't limit faculty evaluation to personnel decisions. Remember, the bedrock reason for evaluation is the improvement of teaching and learning. All other reasons are collateral.

Selecting the Evaluation Instruments. Instead of reinventing the wheel, institutions desirous of introducing an evaluation program should look over those programs now operating successfully at other institutions. Adaptation of an existing program is the better route. It saves time, energy, and stands in closer proximity to success since it borrows from a successful program. One caution: adapt, don't adopt. Modify whatever is necessary to tailor the program to local conditions. The process of adaptation is relatively simple.

Discussing Expectations. Each professor must know what is expected of him. He should meet with his chairman yearly to discuss what constitutes satisfactory and exemplary performance. The meeting should yield agreement on the criteria, and their weights, for the professor's evaluation. The agreement should be consonant with the institutional and departmental goals. The agreement should also include the yardsticks which will show how the professor fared in meeting the agreed on performance standards.

Should the professor fail in serious respects to meet the standards, his failure should be discussed with him far in advance of his termination. He should, also in advance of tenure and retention decisions, be given every opportunity to grow in ways mutually acceptable to him and the institution. While he is to be encouraged to engage in committee work and other professional activities, it must not be to the detriment of his teaching. A balance must be struck that works to best common advantage, professor, institution, students, community. This is an individual balance for each professor that must be carefully explored in yearly consultation with his chairman.

Training the Evaluators. Many professors find themselves in alien territory when asked to appraise their colleagues' performance. For this task they need training, or at least a few orientation sessions. It is axiomatic that the better the training the better the evaluators.

161

Thus, professors should be taught: a) what to look for, b) how to use the evaluation instruments, c) how to work together with other evaluators, d) how results will be used, e) how faculty evaluation leads to faculty development, f) the function and responsibilities of the evaluator, g) recent research findings on faculty evaluation, h) the mechanics of the program, i) how faculty evaluation is part of the institution's comprehensive evaluation of deans, chairmen and other staff members. Training of professors is best effectuated on campus by colleagues highly respected for their solid knowledge of the particular program on the campus and faculty evaluation in general.

Administering the Rating Forms. Many faculty evaluation programs falter because of defective administrative machinery. The most prevalent defects include an irregular rating schedule, bias resulting from flawed instructions, inconsistent or inadequate standards, poorly constructed rating forms. A suggested first step is a dry run to gain needed experience in the construction and administration of rating forms. The dry run has the added advantage of stimulating faculty thinking about the content of the forms and suggesting desirable modifications. In the shakedown unforeseen bugs in administering the forms can also be corrected. The experience adds substantially to the success potential of the program.

It can help, for example, to decide if a single rating form or multiple rating forms should be used by students at the institution. A single rating form offers the enticement of professor comparison throughout the department and the institution. But the single rating form can be treacherous in small or laboratory classes and may be inappropriate given certain campus policies, practices or politics. The dry run helps suggest the answer from institution to institution.

There is a danger of overkill. If the faculty evaluation program requires a professor to self-appraise his performance every semester in every class, the quality of his responses will probably nosedive. Additionally, an appraisal of a professor's performance need be no more frequent than every year or two.

Applying the Evaluation Data. When the purpose of ratings is to improve performance, it is advantageous to issue rating forms to students, faculty colleagues and the to-be-appraised professor early in the term, not at the end of the term. Five weeks into the term is suggested. With the rating results in hand, the professor's performance can thereafter be monitored and deficiencies corrected. Caution: performance improvement is strictly contingent on frank, sympathetic discussion of ratings with the professor by a respected peer.

When ratings are used for personnel decisions, the forms should be completed within the last two weeks of the semester. Caution: the professor's entire performance, including teaching, research, publication, committee work, student advising, other professional activities, must be assessed several times over several semesters by several evaluators before acceptance as reliable data by the program. As the old saw goes, one swallow does not a summer make. One class, one semester, one classroom observation, one evaluator, may do gross injustice to the reality of the professor's performance.

Novice professors should be appraised once each semester but less frequently as they gain experience and their performance is acceptable. At no time and under no circumstances should a single appraisal justify a tenure, promotion or retention decision.

Avoiding the Teaching vs. Research Dilemma. In the hallowed reward system, particularly at the larger, prestigious institutions, the campus eclat is reserved much more for research and publication than for teaching. As a result, a professor who is an outstanding classroom teacher not infrequently finds himself no better off than one whose performance is merely adequate. The difference is the research and publication that has raised the level of a mediocre teacher to near-excellence. There is more than an element of truth in the wry notion that a professor is paid to teach but is evaluated in terms of his research and publication.

This condition has developed in part because of the pervasive belief that the professor must be more than a teacher. He must be a scholar pushing back the frontiers of knowledge and understanding in his discipline. The other side of the coin, the negative side, which also has powered the publish-or-perish dictum, is the belief, held by many administrators and faculty, that teaching does not lend itself to appraisal. It can not, and should not, be appraised. Teaching is so individual that "the good teacher" defies definition. It is so individual, the argument goes, that it is incapable of being measured by standardized instruments. It is largely taken for granted as implicit in the title *professor.*

Actually, teaching can be assessed as rigorously as research and publication and it has been for years by many institutions. How? From student ratings, classroom visits, colleague reviews of teaching materials, alumni opinions, self-assessments, special incidents. A composite three-dimensional professor emerges from the weighted data from these sources that closely approximates the actual professor. Granted, the process has flaws but it is reasonably workable and will serve until it is further improved.

The traditional conflict between research/publication and teaching is of dubious validity. What is most needed are two different tests that can separately and reliably measure excellence in research/publication and in classroom teaching. What is also needed is recognition in the traditional reward system not only of superior research/publication but also of teaching.

Evaluating the Program. The evaluation program must be so designed as to include an internal feedback mechanism for purpose of regular review. It is of comfort to a professor to know that his evaluative process is steadily undergoing review and possible unfair elements are being corrected. It adds to his confidence in, and support of, the evaluative process. It is essential that the mechanics of the review be spelled out in advance in detail.

The review can be informal or it can include an analysis of performance goals and standards and depth interviews with students, colleagues, administrators. The kind of review depends on the local campus needs, politics, and traditions. But whichever review is selected, it must result in close monitoring and, when necessary, in reforms of the evaluation program to enhance its utility and integrity. Publicizing the reforms lends added credibility.

The Matter of Subjective Judgment. Although on first thought it appears that the evaluation system should rest entirely on a quantified, objective analysis, on second thought there is an area in the system that is probably best left to subjective judgment. Unquestionably, tenure, promotion and retention decisions should be based on objective data. But the purpose of the objective data is to help shape a subjective decision. The data are simply means not ends. The system that bans human judgment invites its own death. Conversely, however, the system that depends exclusively on human judgment invites tyranny. Perhaps best is to confine the area of human judgment and depend on open decisions openly arrived at to keep the system honest.

Granted, that current systems of faculty evaluation are imperfect. So are many of the world's systems. The future requires that we continue to improve them.

Maintenance of the Program. The operation of a faculty evaluation program means coping with constant problems year after year. Some of the problems are unnecessary. For example, extravagant demands on students for ratings will tend to diminish their ardor for the program. The same result will come about if students are led to believe their ratings are barely and perfunctorily used. Sometimes a problem will develop inexplicably. One group of students may operate the rating system superbly, a succeeding group may allow it to disintegrate. Some faculty members may balk at the huge expenditure of time and energy required by a classroom observation program. Some may dislike the task of reviewing a colleague's teaching materials. Some may find self-assessment the equivalent of self-torture.

These and other problems require for their solution continuity of the faculty and the active support of the administration. Sympathetic and understanding faculty, administration, students, working together in a cooperative venture, works best.

Grievance Procedures. Every evaluation program whose results apply to tenure, promotion, salary or retention decisions must include a grievance mechanism. It is wise to set up two committees, one to hear procedural and the other substantive grievances. Contingent on local needs, the committees can be either exclusively faculty or faculty with representation by students and administrators. Most important, the grievance procedures must be detailed in advance as part of the faculty evaluation program. An appellate procedure must be available. Since group decisions are generally more acceptable, the committee's decision should be appealed to the faculty senate or the board of trustees rather than to the president or academic vice-president.

Legal Considerations. Few institutions in recent years have been lucky enough to escape lawsuits by professors who have been denied tenure, promotion or contract renewal. In today's legal environment, the casual methods still used to appraise faculty at some institutions have been found wanting and, in many court decisions, illegal. Today, with civil rights legislation on the books together with affirmative action clauses, the inadequate or biased systems of data-collection and interpretations are being increasingly challenged in court. A steadily increasing number of institutions have been judged in violation of law and have been ordered by the court to reverse administrative decisions.

Thus, it is the height of prudence for colleges and universities to scrutinize their faculty evaluation programs and erase inequities before the court orders it done. Following are some suggested guidelines.

1. Administrators, faculty and students should each contribute significantly to the construction of the evaluation program and its performance standards.

2. A careful appraisal of faculty performance must be the basis for every personnel decision.

3. The components of the evaluation program must be job-related and subject to empirical validation.

4. The administration and scoring of the evaluations must be standardized.

5. Multiple evaluation sources are required and each source's appraisal is to be pursued independently.

6. Student evaluations containing comments about professors must not be summarized. Either all or none of the comments should be made public.

7. Classroom observation by colleagues must follow a list of

teaching behaviors previously discussed with the professors being observed.

8. Self-appraisals must not be used for tenure, promotion and retention decisions.

9. Evaluation forms must be written in clear and concise language.

10. Evaluators must be adequately trained.

11. The criteria and procedures used in the evaluation program must be fully understood by the entire faculty.

12. The evaluation program must not only contain no bias but also give no appearance of containing bias.

A Final Word. There are probably more questions about evaluating faculty performance today than there are answers. This makes for difficulty in giving advice, despite urgent requests. But from experience we know a few things.

1. We know there is no perfect system of evaluation. Performance appraisal is an art involving value judgments. A completely reliable and valid system of appraisal may always remain beyond human reach. But with enough time, effort and goodwill, reasonable approximations are reachable.

2. We know that any worthwhile program recognizes faculty appraisal as part of a larger appraisal system, and acknowledges the professor's role in the department, the faculty and the institution.

3. We know that solidly constructed evaluation programs provide each professor with factual information on his strengths and weaknesses, and encourage consultations with faculty improvement specialists (or colleagues with required expertise) to improve his teaching performance.

4. We know that many professors have legitimate fears that evaluation results will be abused by misapplication to tenure, promotion and retention decisions.

5. We know that the combined appraisals of students, faculty colleagues, administrators and the professors' self-assessments are required for reasonably reliable and valid performance judgments.

6. We know that the cornerstone of any evaluation program is its acceptance by the faculty, which depends in turn on the faculty's confidence in the program's relevance, utility, integrity.

7. We know that faculty appraisal is an evolving program and that any component, for example student ratings, may be fashionable this year and obsolete next year.

8. We know that faculty evaluation is only a means to an end - the improvement of teaching in order to improve student learning.

166

Bibliography

Aleamoni, L.M. Typical faculty concerns about student evaluation of instruction. An address at the Technion-Israel Institute of Technology, Haifa, Israel, March 24, 1974.

Alexander, L., B. Elsom, R. Means, and R. Means. Achievement as a function of teacher initiated student-teacher personal interaction. Paper presented at the Annual Meeting of the Southwestern Psychological Association, 1971.

American Academy of Arts and Sciences, Assembly on University Goals and Guidance. *A First Report*. Cambridge, Massachusetts, 1971.

Astin, Alexander. *Preventing Students from Dropping Out*. San Francisco: Jossey-Bass, 1975.

Bayley, D.H. Making college teaching a profession. *Improving College and University Teaching*. *15* (1967), 115-119.

Beaird, J.H. Colleague appraisal of faculty performance. *Professorial Assessment in Higher Education*, eds. C.S. Frost and G.L. Thorne. Monmouth: Oregon State System of Higher Education, 1975.

Behling, R., and C.M. Merz. Student perception of teaching effectiveness. *AACSB Bulletin*, *2*(2), October 1975.

Bendig, A.W. An introverted factor analysis study of student rated introductory psychology instructors. *Journal of Experimental Education*, *21*, 1953, 333-336.

Berkshire, J.R., and R.W. Highland. Forced-choice performance rating—a methodological study. *Personnel Psychology*, *6*, 1953, 356-372.

Berquist, W.H., and S.R. Phillips. *A Handbook for Faculty Development*. Washington, D.C.: Council for the Advancement of Small Colleges, 1975.

Blackburn, Robert. The professor's role in a changing society. ERIC Clearinghouse on Higher Education, Report No. 10, (June, 1971).

Bligh, Donald. *Teaching Students*. Devon, England: Exeter University Teaching Services, 1975.

Bourgeois, D.P. A study of faculty opinion concerning selected factors related to excellence in teaching at the University of Southwestern Louisiana. Unpublished Master's thesis. Lafayette: University of Southwestern Louisiana, 1967.

Braunstein, D.N., and C.J. Benston. Student and department chairman views of the performance of university professors. *Journal of Applied Psychology,* 58, 1973, 244-249.

Bresler, J.B. Teaching effectiveness and government awards. *Science, 160,* 1968, 164-167.

Brock, Stephen. Measuring faculty advisor effectiveness. *Exchange.* Center for Faculty Evaluation and Development, Kansas State University, 1978.

Buhl, L.C., and S.H. Lane. A quantity and quality model for faculty evaluation. In *Proceedings of the Third International Conference on Improving University Teaching,* ed. B.T. Massey. Newcastle, England: University of Maryland, 1977.

Caffrey, B. Luck of bias in student evaluation of teachers. *Proceedings of the 77th Annual Convention of the American Psychological Association, 4,* 1969, 641-642.

Caplow, T., and Reece J. McGee. *The Academic Marketplace.* New York: Basic Books, 1958.

Centra, J.A. Colleagues as raters of classroom instruction. *Journal of Higher Education, 46*(1), 1975, 327-337.

————. The how and why of evaluating teaching. *New Directions for Higher Education,* ed. J.A. Centra. Vol. 17, Spring 1977.

————. How universities evaluate faculty performance: a survey of department heads. Princeton: Educational Testing Service, July 1977.

————. The relationship between student and alumni rating of teachers. *Educational and Psychological Measurement, 34*(2), 1974, 321-326.

————. Self-ratings of college teachers: a comparison with student ratings. *Research Bulletin* 72-33. Princeton: Educational Testing Service, 1972.

————. Student ratings of instruction and their relationship to student learning. *Research Bulletin* 76-6. Princeton: Educational Testing Service, 1976.

————. *The Utility of Student Ratings for Instructional Improvement.* Princeton: Educational Testing Service, 1972.

Choy, Chunghoon. "The relationship of college teacher effectiveness to conceptual systems orientation and perceptual orientation." Unpublished doctoral dissertation, Colorado State College, 1969.

Clark, M.J., and R.T. Blackburn. Assessment of faculty performance: some correlates between self, colleagues, students and administrators. Center for Study of Higher Education, University of Michigan, 1971. (Mimeographed.)

Cohen, A.M., and F.B. Brawer. *Measuring Faculty Performance*. Washington, D.C.: ERIC Clearinghouse for Junior College Information, American Association of Junior Colleges, 1969.

Cohen, J., and L.G. Humphreys. Memorandum to faculty. University of Illinois, Department of Psychology, 1960. (Mimeographed.)

Cohen, S.A., and W.A. Berger. Dimensions of students' ratings of college instructors underlying subsequent achievement in course examinations. *Proceedings of the 78th Annual Convention of the American Psychological Association, 5*, 1970, 605-606.

Corney, William, and Curt Norton. Student advisement: an alternative approach. *Improving College and University Teaching Yearbook 1975*, ed. Delmer Goode. Corvallis, Oregon: Oregon State University Press, 1975.

Costin, F. A graduate course in the teaching of psychology: description and evaluation. *Journal of Teacher Education. 19*, 1968, 425-432.

_____. "Intercorrelation between Students' and Course Chairmen's Ratings of Instructors." University of Illinois, Division of General Studies, 1966. (mimeographed.)

_____, W.T. Greenough, and R.J. Menges. Student ratings of college teaching: reliability, validity and usefulness. *Review of Educational Research. 41*, 1971, 511-535.

Crockett, David. Making advising work: basic elements in developing and implementing a successful academic advising program. *Proceedings of the First Annual Conference on Academic Advising*, ed. Toni Trombley. Burlington, Vermont, October, 1977.

Crow, M.L. UTA faculty survey data released. *INSIGHT to Teaching Excellence, 6*(2), February 1979, 1-7.

Dent, P.L., and D.J. Lewis. The relationship between teaching effectiveness and measures of research quality. *Educational Research Quarterly. 1*(3), Fall 1976, 3-16.

Donald, Janet G., and Bruce Shore. Student learning and the evaluation of teaching. *If Teaching is Important . . . The Evaluation of Instruction in Higher Education*, ed. C.K. Knapper. Ottowa: Clarke, Irwin and Co., 1977.

Downie, N.W. Student evaluation of faculty. *Journal of Higher Education. 23*, 1952, 495-496.

Drake, H.A. No points for teaching: the evaluation dilemma. *INSIGHT to Teaching Excellence, 3*(3), February 1976, 1-6.

Doyle, K.O., Jr. *Student Evaluation of Instruction*. Lexington, Massachusetts: Lexington Books, D.C Heath and Co., 1975.

169

Dressel, P. The current status of research in college and university teaching. *The Appraisal of Teaching in Large Universities*, ed. W.J. McKeachie. Ann Arbor: University of Michigan, 1959.

————. Evaluation of the environment, the process, and the results of higher education. *Handbook of College and University Administration: Academic*, ed. A.S. Knowles. New York: McGraw Hill, 1970.

Druckers, A.J., and H.H. Remmers. Do alumni and students differ in their attitudes toward instructors? *Journal of Educational Psychology*. 42(3), 1951, 129-143.

Dubin, B., and T.C. Taveggia. *The Teaching-Learning Paradox: A Comparative Analysis of College Teaching Methods*. Eugene, Oregon: University of Oregon, Center for the Advanced Study of Educational Administration, 1968.

Dunkin, M.J., and B.J. Biddle. *The Study of Teaching*. New York: Holt, Rinehart and Winston, 1974.

Dwyer, F.M. Selected criteria for evaluating teacher effectiveness. *Improving College and University Teaching*. 21(1), 1974, 51-52.

Eble, K.E. *The Craft of Teaching*. San Francisco: Jossey-Bass, 1976.

————. *Professors as Teachers*. San Francisco: Jossey-Bass, 1972.

————. Project to Improve College Teaching. *Academe*, 4, 1970, 3-6.

————. *The Recognition and Evaluation of Teaching*. Salt Lake City: Project to Improve College Teaching, 1970.

Education Directory. Washington, D.C.: Government Printing Office, 1977.

Elliott, D.N. Characteristics and relationships of various criteria of college and university teaching. *Perdue University Studies in Higher Education*. 70, 1950, 5-61.

Erickson, S.C. Student evaluation of teaching. *Criteria*. Center for Research on Learning and Teaching, University of Michigan. No. 2, June 1976.

Estrin, H.A., and L.R. Godwin. Evaluating English teaching. *Improving College and University Teaching*. 10, 1962, 193-196.

Finlayson, Elizabeth. The preparation and use of a handbook for academic advising. *Proceedings of the First Annual Conference on Academic Advising*, ed. Toni Trombley. Burlington, Vermont, October, 1977.

Fisk, Edward. *The New York Times*. March 12, 1978, p. 9.

Flewellen, W.C. Faculty evaluation: the University of Georgia case. *Professorial Assessment in Higher Education*, eds. C.S. Scott and G.L. Thorne. Monmouth: Oregon State System of Higher Education, 1975.

————. Personal communication. March 16, 1979.

Follman, T., D.L. Lantz, and E.C. Anderson. *Teaching versus*

170

Research. Washington, D.C.: American Psychological Association Research Monograph, 1973.

Fordham University Faculty of Business. "Deliberations of the Task Force on Merit Increase Awards." New York, 1979. (Mimeographed.)

Frankel, C. Rights and responsibility of the student-college relationship. *The College and University Student*, eds. L.E. Dennis, and J.F. Kauffman. Washington, D.C.: American Council on Education, 1965.

Gaff, J. Teachers who make a difference. *Proceedings of the First Invitational Conference on Faculty Effectiveness as Evaluated by Students*, ed. A. Sockcoff. Philadelphia: Temple University, 1973.

_____, and Robert C. Wilson. *New Teaching, New Learning*, ed. Kerry Smith. Washington, D.C.: American Association for Higher Education. Jossey-Bass, 1971.

Gage, N.L. The appraisal of college teaching. *Journal of Higher Education*, 32, 1961, 17-22.

_____. Students' rating of college teaching: their justification and proper use. *Second OCSB Conference on Effective Teaching*, eds. N.S. Glasman and B.R. Killait, 1974, 79-86.

Garwood, John. Improving instruction. Ft. Hays State University, No. 16, September 1978.

Goldstein, R.J., and R.C. Anderson. Attitudes of faculty toward teaching. *Improving College and University Teaching*, 25(2), Spring 1977, 110-111.

Goodhartz, A.S. Student attitudes and opinions relating to teaching at Brooklyn College. *School and Society*. 68, 1948, 345-349.

Granger, Rebecca. Student attitudes toward teaching improvement. *PIRIT* (Project on Institutional Renewal through the Improvement of Teaching) *Newsletter*. No. 3, June 1977.

Grasha, A.F. *Assessing and Developing Faculty Performance*. Cincinnati, Ohio: Communication and Education Associates, 1977.

Grites, Thomas, and Joseph Metz. Developing a model for academic advising. *Proceedings of the First Annual Conference on Academic Advising*, ed. Toni Trombley. Burlington, Vermont, October 1977.

_____, and _____. Maximizing the use of faculty advisors. *Proceedings of the First Annual Conference on Academic Advising*, ed. Toni Trombley. Burlington, Vermont, October 1977.

Gromisch, D.S. A comparison of student and departmental chairmen evaluations of teaching performance. *Journal of Medical Education*. 47, 1972, 281-284.

The Group for Human Development in Higher Education. *Faculty Development in a Time of Retrenchment.* New Rochelle, New York: Change Magazine, 1974.

Gustad, J.W. *Policies and practices in faculty evaluation.* Washington, D.C.: Committee on College Teaching, American Council on Education, 1961.

————. Policies and practices in faculty evaluation. *The Educational Record.* July 1961, pp. 195-211.

Report of the task force on pedagogical improvement. Cambridge: Harvard University, 1977.

Harvey, J.N., and D.G. Barker. Student evaluation of teaching effectiveness. *Improving College and University Teaching. 18,* 1970, 275-278.

Hayes, J.R. Research, teaching and faculty fate. *Science, 172,* 1971, 227-230.

Heilman, J.D., and W.D. Armentrout. The rating of college teachers on ten traits by their students. *Journal of Educational Psychology, 27,* 1936, 197-216.

Heiss, A.M. "The Utilization of the College and University Teacher." Berkeley: Center for Research and Development in Higher Education, 1968. (Mimeographed.)

Heywood, J. Qualification, teaching and industrial experience of some staff in five colleges of advanced technology. *Industrial Journal of Electrical Engineering Education, 5,* 699-705.

Hildebrand, M. How to recommend promotion for a mediocre teacher without actually lying. *Professorial Assessment in Higher Education,* eds. C.S Scott and G.L. Thorne. Monmouth: Oregon State System of Higher Education, 1975.

————, R.C. Wilson, and E.R. Dienst. *Evaluating University Teaching.* Berkeley: University of California, Center for Research and Development in Higher Education, 1971.

Hoyt, D.P. *Improving Instruction through Student Feedback.* Manhattan, Kansas: Kansas State University, 1969.

————. Instructional effectiveness—interrelationship with publication record and monetary reward. Research report #10. Kansas State University, Office of Educational Research, May 1970.

Irby, D.M. Clinical faculty development. *Clinical Education for the Allied Health Professions,* ed. C. Ford. St. Louis: C.V. Mosby Company, 1978.

Jencks, C., and D. Riesman. *The Academic Revolution.* Garden City, New York: Doubleday, 1969.

Kent, L. Student evaluation of teaching. *Improving College Teaching,* ed. C.B.T. Lee. Washington, D.C.: American Council on Education, 1967.

172

Kestin, J. Reflections on the teaching of engineering at a university. *American Scientist. 51*, 1963, 437.

Kirchner, R.P. A central factor in teacher evaluation by students. Unpublished research paper, Lexington: University of Kentucky, 1969.

Knapper, C.K. Evaluation and teaching: beyond lip-service. *Proceedings on the Fourth International Conference on Improving University Teaching*, ed. B.T. Massey. Aachen, Germany: University of Maryland, 1978.

Kohlan, R.G. A comparison of faculty evaluations early and late in the course. *Journal of Higher Education. 44*, 1973, 587-594.

Kramer, Howard. Faculty advising: a part of faculty development. *Exchange*. Center for Evaluation and Development in Higher Education, Kansas State University. December 1978.

Kulik, J.A. Memo to the faculty. The University of Michigan. No. 53, February 1974.

Ladd, E.C., Jr., and S.M. Lipset. Ladd-Lipset survey. *The Chronicle of Higher Education, 15*(12), November 21, 1977, 2.

_____, and _____. What do professors like best about their jobs? *The Chronicle of Higher Education*, March 29, 1976, 10.

_____, and _____. How professors spend their time. *The Chronicle of Higher Education, 11*(5), October 27, 1975, 2.

Langen, T.D. Student assessment of teaching effectiveness. *Improving College and University Teaching, 13*(1), Winter 1966, 25.

Lathrop, R.G. "Unit Factorial Ratings by College Students of Courses and Instructors." Chico State College, California, 1968. (Mimeographed.)

Levesque, G.A. Publish, yea, even if it be thy doctoral dissertation. *The Chronicle of Higher Education*, September 19, 1977, 32.

Linsky, A.S., and M.A. Strauss. Student evaluations, research productivity, and eminence of college faculty. *Journal of Higher Education, 46*, 1975, 89-101.

Lovell, G.D., and C.F. Haner. Forced-choice applied to college faculty rating. *Educational and Psychology Measurement, 15*, 1955, 291-304.

Magarrell, J. Inflation hit colleges harder in fiscal 1978. *The Chronicle of Higher Education, 17*(4), September 25, 1978.

Mager, R.F. *Preparing Instructional Objectives*, 2nd edition. Palo Alto, California: Belmont, 1978.

Mangold, Charlotte W. Advisement as a factor in student performance. *Proceedings of the Fourth International Conference on Improving University Teaching*, ed. Benjamin T. Massey. Aachen, Germany: University of Maryland, 1972.

173

Mannan, G., and E.M. Traicoff. Evaluation of an ideal university teacher. *Improving College and University Teaching*, 24(2), Spring 1976, 98-101.

Marsh, H.W., and S.P. Kesler. *The Validity of Student Evaluations: A Comparison of Faculty Self-Evaluations and Student Evaluations*. Los Angeles: University of Southern California, Office of Institutional Studies, 1976.

Maslow, A.H., and W. Zimmerman. College teaching ability, scholarship, activity and personality. *Journal of Educational Psychology*, 47, 1956, 185-189.

McDaniel, E.D., and J.F. Feldhusen. Relationships between faculty ratings and indexes of service and scholarship. *Proceedings of the 78th Annual Convention of the American Psychological Association*. 5, 1970, 619-620.

McGrath, E.J. Characteristics of outstanding college teachers. *Journal of Higher Education*, 33, 1962, 148.

McGrath, N. Many researchers not on faculties. *The Chronicle of Higher Education*, 17(19), 19.

McIntyre, C.J. Evaluation of college teachers. *Criteria, 6*, May 1977.

McKeachie, W.J. Assessing teaching effectiveness: comments and summary. *Proceedings of the First International Conference on Improving University Teaching*, ed. B. Massey. Heidelberg: University of Maryland, 1975.

_____. Research in teaching: the gap between theory and practice, ed. C.B.T. Lee. *Improving College Teaching*. Washington, D.C.: American Council on Education, 1967.

_____. *Teaching Tips*. Lexington, Massachusetts: D.C. Heath and Company, 1978.

_____, and J.A. Kulik. Effective college teaching. *Review of Research in Education*, ed. F. Kerlinger. Vol. 3. ITASCA, Illinois: Peacock, 1975.

_____, Y. Lin, and W. Mann. Student ratings of teacher effectiveness: validity studies. *American Educational Research Journal*. 8, 1971, 435-445.

McMartin, J.A., and H.E. Rich. Faculty opinion at California State University, Northridge, Toward student evaluation of teaching effectiveness. Unpublished research paper.

Megaw, Neill. The dynamics of evaluation. *Improving College Teaching*, ed. C.B.T. Lee. Washington, D.C.: American Council on Education, 1967.

Melnick, M., and P. Adams. Teaching improvement programs in post-secondary education. *Reform, Renewal, Reward*, ed. D.W. Allen. Amherst: University of Massachusetts, 1975.

Menges, R.J. The new reporters, students rule instruction. *Evaluating Learning and Teaching, New Directions in Higher*

Education, ed. C.R. Pace. San Francisco: Jossey-Bass, 1973.

Middleton, Lorenzo. With freshmen scarcer, emphasis shifts to keeping present students. *The Chronicle of Higher Education,* 17(9), October 30, 1978, 1.

Miller, M.T. Instructor attitudes toward, and the use of, student ratings of teachers. *Journal of Educational Psychology, 62,* 1971, 235-239.

Miller, R.I. Assessing teacher effectiveness. *Proceedings of the First International Conference on Improving University Teaching,* ed. B. Massey. Heidelberg: University of Maryland, 1975.

_____. *Evaluating Faculty Performance.* San Francisco: Jossey-Bass, 1972.

_____. *Developing Programs for Faculty Evaluation.* San Francisco: Jossey-Bass, 1974.

Milton, O. *Alternatives to the Traditional.* San Francisco: Jossey-Bass, 1972.

Mooman, N.E. *Faculty Evaluation for Improved Learning.* Atlanta: Southern Regional Education Board, 1977.

Morton, R.K. Evaluating college teaching. *Improving College and University Teaching,* 9, 1961, 122-123.

Murray, H.G. The reliability and validity of student ratings of faculty teaching ability. Unpublished manuscript, 1973.

Nadeau, Gilles. Student evaluation of instruction: the rating questionnaire. *If Teaching is Important . . . the Evaluation of Instruction in Higher Education,* ed. C.K. Knapper. Ottawa, Canada: Irwin and Company, Limited, 1977.

Naftulin, D.H., J.E. Ware, and F.A. Donnelly. The Dr. Fox lecture: a paradigm of educational seduction. *Journal of Medical Education,* 48, 1973, 630-635.

Netusil, A.J., and D.A. Hallenbeck. Assessing perceptions of college student satisfaction. *NASPA Journal, 12,* Spring 1975, 263-267.

The student learning scales. *NU News,* Brief Report #3. University of Nebraska, April 1978.

Ozmon, H. Publications and teaching. *Improving College and University Teaching, 15,* 1967, 106-107.

Pambookian, H.S. "The Effect of Feedback from Students to College Instructors on their Teaching Behavior." Unpublished Doctoral dissertation, University of Michigan, 1972.

_____. Feedback to instructors on their teaching to improve instruction. *Proceedings of the Third International Conference on Improving University Teaching,* ed. B. Massey. England: University of Maryland, 1977.

Piper, D.W. What makes teaching effective? An occasional paper. London: University of London, Teaching Methods Unit, 1977.

Priest, B.J. Classroom: castles or learning laboratories. *Improving*

College Teaching, ed. C.B.T. Lee. Washington, D.C.: American Council on Education, 1967.

Quinn, M.R. Designing an effective faculty evaluation program. *Journal of Business Education,* May 1978, pp. 343-347.

Remmers, H.H. *Manual of Instruction for the Perdue Rating Scale of Instructors* (Rev. ed.). West Lafayette, Indiana: University Book Store, 1960.

_____. On Students' Perceptions of Teachers' Effectiveness. *The Appraisal of Teaching in Large Universities,* ed. W.J. McKeachie. Ann Arbor: University of Michigan Extension Service, 1959.

Rezler, A.G., and A.S. Anderson. Focused and unfocused feedback and self-perception. *The Journal of Educational Research, 65,* October 1971, 61-64.

Riley, J.W., B.F. Ryan, and M. Lifschitz. *The Student Looks at His Teacher.* New Brunswick: Rutgers University Press, 1950.

Rodin, Miriam. Rating the teachers. *The Center Magazine.* 8(5), September/October 1975, 55-60.

_____, and B. Rodin. Student evaluations of teachers. *Science, 177,* September 29, 1972, 1164-1166.

Rose, C. Faculty evaluation in an accountable world. *Faculty Development and Evaluation in Higher Education.* 2(2), Summer 1976.

Rosovsky, H. *Report of the task force on pedagogical improvement.* Cambridge: Harvard University, May 12, 1977.

Rossman, J.E. Teaching, publication and rewards at a liberal arts college. *Improving College and University Teaching, 24*(4), Fall 1976, 238-240.

Salter, B. Can we break the powerful myths about research? *The London Times Higher Education Supplement,* November 25, 1977.

Sanford, Neville. Academic culture and the teacher's development. *Soundings,* 1971, pp. 357-371.

Sargent, Harold Ross. Administration and faculty self-evaluation. *Education, 95*(1), 72-75.

Sayer, S., and A.G. Harding. The assessment of teaching effectiveness, end or mean? *Proceedings of the First International Conference on Improving University Teaching,* ed. B. Massey. Heidelberg: University of Maryland, 1975.

Scott, Craig. Collecting information about student learning. *Professorial Assessment in Higher Education,* eds. C.S. Scott and G.C. Thorne. Monmouth: Oregon State System of Higher Education, 1975.

_____. Student input relative to professorial performance. *Professorial Assessment in Higher Education,* eds. C.S. Scott and G.C. Thorne. Monmouth: Oregon State System of Higher

Education, 1975.

Seldin, Peter. Faculty growth contracts. Occasional paper. London: University of London, Institute of Education, 1977.

_____. *How Colleges Evaluate Professors.* New York: Blythe— Pennington, Ltd., 1975.

_____. Rating the teachers. *The Center Magazine*, 8(6), November/December 1975, 75-76.

_____. *Teaching Professors to Teach.* New York: Blythe— Pennington, Ltd., 1977.

Simpson, R.H., and J.M. Seidman. Use of teacher self-evaluation tools for the improvement of instruction. Paper presented at the American Association of Colleges for Teacher Education conference, 1962.

Skipper, Charles E. A technique for teacher self-evaluation. *Improving College and University Teaching Yearbook*, ed. Delmer Goode. Corvallis, Oregon: Oregon State University Press, 1975.

Smart, R.C. The evaluation of teaching performance from the point of view of the teaching profession. Paper presented at the American Psychological Association meeting, Chicago, 1975.

Solomon, D. Teacher behavior dimensions, course characteristics, and student evaluation of teachers. *American Educational Research Journal*, 3, 1966, 35-47.

Sorey, K.E. A study of the distinguishing personality characteristics of college faculty who are superior in regard to the teaching function. *Dissertation Abstracts*, 28(12-A), 1968, 4916.

Spencer, R.E. The Illinois course evaluation questionnaire: manual of interpretation. Research report No. 270. Champaign: University of Illinois, 1968.

_____, and L.M. Aleamoni. A student course evaluation questionnaire. *Journal of Educational Measurement*, 7, 1970, 209-210.

Stallings, W.M., and S. Singhal. Some observations on the relationship between research productivity and student evaluation of courses and teaching. *AERA Paper Abstracts*, ed. V. Crockenberg. Washington, D.C.: American Educational Research Association, 1969.

Starr, Robert J., Research into practice: some guidelines for evaluating teaching in higher education. *Proceedings of the Fourth International Conference on Improving University Teaching*, ed. B. Massey. Aachen, Germany: University of Maryland, 1978.

Statement on teaching evaluation. *AAUP Bulletin*, 60(2), 1974, 166-170.

Striner, H.E. "Memo to All Full-Time SBA Faculty Members." The

American University. April 2, 1977. (Mimeographed.)
_____. Personal communication. April 12, 1979.
Sullivan, A.M., and G.R. Skanes. Validity of student evaluation of teaching and the characteristics of successful instructors. *Journal of Educational Psychology, 66*(4), 1974, 584-590.
TDR Associates. *Mutual Benefit Evaluation of Faculty and Administrators in Higher Education.* Newton: Massachusetts Advisory Council on Education, 1975.
Editorial. Institutionalized research or individual scholarship. *The Times Higher Education Supplement.* London, No.323. January 13, 1978.
Toug, M.S., and T.F. Feldhusen. The relationship between student ratings of instructors and their particupation in classroom discussion. Paper presented at the meeting of the National Council on Measurement in Education. New Orleans, February, 1973.
_____, _____, and J. Halstead. Criterion-reference validity of student ratings. Paper read at annual meeting of the American Educational Research Association, 1973.
Trent, J., and A. Cohen. Research on teaching in higher education. *Second Handbook of Research on Teaching,* ed. R. Travers. Chicago: Rand McNally, 1973.
Tuckman, Bruce W. Teaching assessment based on learning outcomes. *Proceedings of the Fourth International Conference on Improving University Teaching,* ed. B.T. Massey. Aachen, Germany: University of Maryland, 1978.
Voeks, V.W. Publications and teaching effectiveness. *Journal of Higher Education, 33,* 1962, 212.
_____, and G.M. French. Are student ratings of teachers affected by grades? *Journal of Higher Education, 31,* 1960, 330-334.
Ware, J.E., and R.G. Williams. The Dr. Fox effect: a study of lecture effectiveness and ratings of instruction. *Journal of Medical Education, 50,* 1975, 149-156.
Weaver, C.H. Instructor ratings by college students. *Journal of Educational Psychology, 51,* 1960, 21-25.
Webb, W.B., and C.Y. Nolan. Student, supervisor, and self-ratings of instructional proficiency. *The Journal of Educational Psychology, 46,* 1955, 42-46.
Williams, R.G., and J.E. Ware. Validity of student ratings of instruction under different incentive conditions: a further study of the Dr. Fox effect. *Journal of Educational Psychology, 68,* 1976, 48-56.
Wilson, W.R. Students rating teachers. *Journal of Higher Education, 3,* 1932, 75-82.

Winthrop, H. Worth of a colleague. *Improving College and University Teaching, 14,* 1966, 262-267.

Wolf, L.G. Letter to the editor. *The Chronicle of Higher Education, 15* (19), p. 16.

Appendix

Part I

EVALUATION OF OVERALL FACULTY PERFORMANCE

Instructions:

What factors are principally considered in evaluating a faculty member for promotion in rank, salary increase or tenure? Please indicate the importance of each factor by placing a circle around <u>one</u> response in each row.

IBM Code / Factors	(1) Major Factor	(2) Minor Factor	(3) Not A Factor	(4) Not Applicable
1. Classroom teaching	1	2	3	4
2. Supervision of graduate study	1	2	3	4
3. Supervision of honors program	1	2	3	4
4. Research	1	2	3	4
5. Publication	1	2	3	4
6. Public service	1	2	3	4
7. Consultation (government, business)	1	2	3	4
8. Activity in professional societies	1	2	3	4
9. Student advising	1	2	3	4
10. Campus committee work	1	2	3	4
11. Length of service in rank	1	2	3	4
12. Competing job offers	1	2	3	4
13. Personal attributes	1	2	3	4
14. Other (specify)	1	2	3	4

EVALUATION OF TEACHING PERFORMANCE

Instructions:

Please indicate the frequency with which each of the following types of information is used in your college in evaluating a faculty member's <u>teaching performance.</u>   (Please circle <u>one</u> answer in each row.)

Types of information	(1) Always Used	(2) Usually Used	(3) Seldom Used	(4) Never Used
15. Systematic student ratings	1	2	3	4
16. Informal student opinions	1	2	3	4
17. Classroom visits	1	2	3	4
18. Colleagues' opinions	1	2	3	4
19. Scholarly research and publication	1	2	3	4
20. Student examination performance	1	2	3	4
21. Chairman evaluation	1	2	3	4
22. Dean evaluation	1	2	3	4
23. Course syllabi and examinations	1	2	3	4
24. Long term follow-up of students	1	2	3	4
25. Enrollment in elective courses	1	2	3	4
26. Alumni opinions	1	2	3	4
27. Committee evaluation	1	2	3	4
28. Grade distributions	1	2	3	4
29. Self evaluation or report	1	2	3	4
30. Other (specify)	1	2	3	4

31. Do you routinely employ any special rating forms or other instruments in collecting data on teaching competence? Please circle the appropriate number.   Yes ___1___ No ___2___
(If yes, please attach copies of these instruments.)

32. Has your institution developed research concerning the validity or usefulness of these instruments? Please circle the appropriate number.   Yes ___1___ No ___2___

Part II

EVALUATION OF SCHOLARSHIP/RESEARCH PERFORMANCE

Instructions:

Please indicate the frequency with which each of the following types of information is used in your college in evaluating a faculty member's scholarship/research performance. (Please circle one answer in each row.)

Types of information	(1) Always Used	(2) Usually Used	(3) Seldom Used	(4) Never Used
33. Publications in all professional journals	1	2	3	4
34. Articles in quality journals	1	2	3	4
35. Unpublished papers or reports	1	2	3	4
36. Papers at professional meetings	1	2	3	4
37. Citations to published materials	1	2	3	4
38. Books as sole or senior author	1	2	3	4
39. Books as junior author or editor	1	2	3	4
40. Monographs or chapters in books	1	2	3	4

Quality of research and publication as judged by:				
41. Peers at the institution	1	2	3	4
42. Peers at other institutions	1	2	3	4
43. Department chairman	1	2	3	4
44. Dean	1	2	3	4
45. Self-evaluations	1	2	3	4
46. Grants or funding received	1	2	3	4
47. Referee or editor of professional journal	1	2	3	4
48. Honors or awards from profession	1	2	3	4
49. Other (specify)	1	2	3	4

Part III

EVALUATION OF COLLEGE SERVICE PERFORMANCE

Instructions:

Please indicate the frequency with which each of the following factors is used in your college in evaluating a faculty member's college service performance. (Please circle one answer in each row.)

Factors	(1) Major Factor	(2) Minor Factor	(3) Not A Factor	(4) Not Applicable
50. Service on department committee	1	2	3	4
51. Service on college-wide committee	1	2	3	4
52. Academic advising	1	2	3	4
53. Non-academic student counseling	1	2	3	4
54. Willingness to teach undesirable courses	1	2	3	4
55. Advisor to student organizations	1	2	3	4
56. Service as student recruiter	1	2	3	4
57. Departmental administrative duties	1	2	3	4
58. Participation in campus symposia	1	2	3	4
59. Other (specify)	1	2	3	4

PERSONAL JUDGEMENT QUESTIONS

Instructions:

Your personal judgment is wanted rather than a report of the on-going policies and practices in your college. Please indicate your reaction to each of the following statements by placing a circle around the answer in each row that most closely reflects your personal judgment.

	Strongly Agree		Strongly Disagree	
60. The results of systematic student evaluation of a faculty member's teaching performance indicate more about a teacher's popularity than about his teaching performance.	1	2	3	4
61. The results of systematic student evaluation of a faculty member's teaching performance should be made public.	1	2	3	4
62. Systematic and planned classroom visitation by faculty colleagues for the purpose of evaluating a faculty member's teaching performance is an invasion of academic privacy.	1	2	3	4
63. Results of an institutionalized, uniform approach to faculty self-evaluation should be one of the important components in evaluation of faculty teaching performance.	1	2	3	4
64. The academic personnel policies and practices used to evaluate a faculty member's teaching performance are well known by most members of the faculty.	1	2	3	4
65. Academic personnel decisions made in liberal arts colleges are based primarily on objective information (that is, information that is rational, impersonal and unprejudiced).	1	2	3	4

College Data: (Please circle the appropriate number for your college.)
66. Institutional control: Private ___1___ Public ___2___
67. Religious affiliation? Yes ___1___ No ___2___

COMMENTS: YOUR COMMENTS ARE INVITED.

182